Redwood Empire

Redwood Empire

by Stuart Nixon

E. P. DUTTON & CO., INC. / NEW YORK 1966

Surf and rocks near mouth of the
Russian River in Sonoma County.

Designed by Jane Byers Bierhorst

Lithographed by The Murray Printing Company,
Forge Village, Massachusetts

Dedicated to the pioneer photographers:
Eadweard Muybridge, Carleton Emmons Watkins,
William Augustus Ericson, Aurelius Ornando Carpenter,
and their contemporaries who roamed the
Redwood Empire with wagon, box camera and
glass plates to record the nineteenth
century for our everlasting wonder

_____

Contents

FOREWORD 11

BEGINNINGS: THE NORTH BAY 21

WINE VALLEYS AND LAKES: THE NAPA VALLEY 65

SOUTH COAST AND RIVERS: SONOMA AND MENDOCINO 93

THE INTERIOR: GUN LAW IN ROUND VALLEY 142

BIG TREE COUNTRY: FIRST PROBERS NORTH 162

THE NORTH COAST: THE LAW BEYOND THE KLAMATH 200

REDWOODS FEED THE FIRES OF CONTROVERSY:

   WHAT PRICE TALL TREES? 216

CATACLYSM: DECEMBER, 1964 234

AN EMPIRE AWAKENING:

   SOME GLIMPSES OF THE FUTURE 248

INDEX 254

*Sonoma Coast: pines and lichens
north of Fort Ross.*

List of Color Plates

Surf and rocks near the mouth of the Russian River
frontispiece

Coast Redwoods beside Bull Creek, in Rockefeller Redwoods State Park
south of Eureka
facing page 24

Lonely stretch of Mendocino Coast north of Westport
facing page 56

Picturesque Noyo, fishing village south of Fort Bragg
facing page 56

Carson Mansion
facing page 88

Log pond at The Pacific Lumber Company Mill, Scotia
facing page 104

After a rain at Bull Creek Flat
facing page 104

Fern Canyon, part of Prairie Creek Redwoods State Park
facing page 144

Sunset, Little River on the Mendocino Coast
facing page 170

Marin County Civic Center
facing page 170

World's tallest living trees, in northern Humboldt County
facing page 218

Water tower and artists' quarters, Mendocino
facing page 232

Old Baptist Church, Mendocino
facing page 232

Deepest appreciation to all those who helped me with Redwood Empire, *including Robert J. Lee, Mrs. Nannie Escola, Harvey J. Hansen, Emmanuel Fritz, Kramer Adams, Bernarr Bates, Jack Craemer, Mrs. Jean Day, Irving Shepard, Mrs. Mathilda Dring, L. D. Dennen, Ole and Cora Hervilla, Tom Knight, Rudy Gillard, J. Dwight O'Dell, Mrs. Percy J. Bryan, Jack Butters, Alan W. Cundall, Robert O. Lee, Richard Childs, Mike Hayden, Dan Bowerman, Bernard J. Vaughn, Dave James, John Robinson, Mrs. Frances H. Purser, Emmy Lou Packard, Mark A. Carpenter, Hector H. Lee, Lester Koritz, Bill Zacha, Dave Hoppe, Alden Ball, Chad H. Hoopes, Vernor Schenck, Doug Wilson, Peter Palmquist, Wallace Martin, Charles Thielen, Leigh Shoemaker, Carney J. Campion, and Florence Taft Nixon. Special thanks to Ansel Adams. Also special thanks to Neil Hulbert, lost en route to Vietnam on March 5, 1966.*

Grateful acknowledgment is made to the following for permission to reproduce the photographs in this book:

Aero Photographers—p. 251. Ansel Adams—pp. 6, 16, 138, 221, 230. Bancroft Library, University of California—pp. 22, 66, 104, 106, 112T, 170, 171; ALSO PHOTO BY: Carleton Emmons Watkins—p. 27T. Mrs. Percy Bryan—pp. 111B, 165, 166, 167, 168, 174, 179B, 180, 183B. Bureau of Land Management—p. 231. California Division of Highways—pp. 158T, 158B, 159T, 159BL, 159BR, 204B. California Historical Society—p. 97T. California Redwood Association—facing p. 24, pp. 95R, 226T, 226B, 227R, 228B; ALSO PHOTOS BY: Morley Baer—p. 31B. Karl H. Riek—p. 250. California State Library—pp. 67B, 70R, 157B, 172L. Richard Childs Collection—pp. 200L, 200R, 206TR, 206B. Alan Cundall—pp. 100B, 101. Cora Coombs Hervilla Collection—p. 105T. *Crescent City American*—pp. 245B, 247T. A. W. Ericson—p. 188T. Eureka Newspapers Inc., photos by: Doug Dill—pp. 237L, 237R, 245T. Dave K. Hoppe—pp. 86, 189T, 229T, 229B. Neil K. Hulbert—pp. 194T, 236, 241B. Doug Wilson—p. 219. Georgia-Pacific Corporation—pp. 216, 227B, 228T. Collection of Roy D. Graves—pp. 30, 90B. Mary Hayden—p. 130T. Mike Hayden—pp. 189B, 192T. *Humboldt Beacon*, photos by: Rudy Gillard—pp. 235, 238, 239T, 239B, 240T, 241T. Humboldt County Historical Society—pp. 164L, 172R. Humboldt State College Library—pp. 178, 179T. Stewart H. Hussey—p. 155. Philip Hyde—pp. 195B, 220. Robert J. Lee Collection—pp. 78B, 80, 107, 111T, 114T, 121, 130B, 148; ALSO PHOTOS BY: A. O. Carpenter—pp. 116T, 116B, 117L, 117R. Marin Historical Society—pp. 31T, 37. Maxwell Galleries—pp. 146, 147TL, 147TR, 147BL, 147BR. Melendy Collection, Humboldt State College—pp. 154, 157T; ALSO PHOTO BY: R. J. Baker—p. 190. Pacific Gas & Electric Company—p. 192B. The Pacific Lumber Company—pp. 181T, 181B, 182T, 182B, 183T. Peter E. Palmquist—pp. 215, 225R, 225BL. Redwood Empire Association—Frontispiece, pp. 26, 29, 33T, 36, 40, 50, 57L, 58B, 59L, 59BR, 60, 61R, 62, 67T, 69T, 69B, 70L, 71, 78M, 79B, 81L, 82R, 83T, 83M, 83B, 84M, 84B, 85L, 85R, 91, 97B, 98L, 98M, 98R, facing p. 104T, facing p. 104B, 123T, 123B, 124, 125T, 125B, 126, 127L, 127M, 127R, 128B, 132T, 133B, 135T, 141T, 141B, 142, 143T, 143B, 145, 149, 150, 151, 153L, 160, 162, 163, 169, facing p. 170T, 187TL, 187TR, 187B, 189M, 198T, 199B, 203BL, 204T, 206TL, 207, 208, 210B, 211B, 223L, 225TL, facing p. 232T, facing p. 232B, 233, 240B, 242, 243T, 243B, 244, 246M, 246B, 247BL, 247BR; ALSO PHOTOS BY: Aero Photographers—pp. 32, 38-39, 79T, facing p. 170B. Ansel Adams—pp. 11, 12, 42, 43, 93, 94, 109, 122, 140, 176, 196, 197, 212, 213, 252, 253. Chuck Davis—p. 87B, 88. Madison Devlin—pp. 74, 76T, 76B, 77T, 77B, 139. Jack Glunk—p. 249. Charles Holbrook—p. 82I. George Knight—p. 25. Burt Levenhagen—p. 34. Hubert Lowman—pp. 18, facing p. 56T, facing p. 56B, 73T, 81R, 87T, 89, 131, 137T. Jack Rice—pp. 47, 54L, 128T, 132B, 133T, 134T. James W. Ross—pp. 35, 41B. David H. Swanlund—facing p. 88, facing p. 144, pp. 161L, 161R, 184, 185, facing p. 218. San Francisco Maritime Museum—pp. 105B, 114B, 115T, 119L, 120T, 191M, 191B, 203BR; ALSO PHOTO BY: Freeman Studios—p. 191T. *San Rafael Independent-Journal*—pp. 24, 33B, 41T. Santa Rosa Junior College Library—pp. 27B, 44, 45T, 45B, 46, 61L, 90T, 95L, 96T, 96B, 97M. *Santa Rosa Press-Democrat*—pp. 63, 99. Save-the-Redwoods League—pp. 214, 217. Sea Ranch, photo by: Ned Westover—p. 102. Irving Shepard Collection—pp. 56, 57R, 58T, 59TR. Tom Shepherd—p. 193T. Simpson Timber Company, photos by: Seely Photos—pp. 205T, 205B. Ron Stammer—pp. 193B, 194B, 198B. David H. Swanlund—pp. 175, 188B, 195T, 232. Kay Trutna—p. 199T. Timber Cove Properties, photos by: Ansel Adams—pp. 8, 100T, 103, 118, 248. Union Lumber Company—pp. 13, 108, 110T, 110B, 115B, 119R, 137B, 222, 223; ALSO PHOTOS BY: W. T. Fitch—p. 112B. Fredericks Studio—p. 113T. University of California Library—p. 186. Wells Fargo Bank, photos by: Ansel Adams—pp. 20, 48, 49, 64-65, 92, 120B. Doug Wilson—pp. 203T, 210T, 211T. Wine Institute—pp. 51, 52T, 52B, 53, 54T, 73B, 75B, 78T, 84T; ALSO PHOTOS BY: Joe Monroe—pp. 72, 75T. Bill Zacha—p. 129.

Foreword

North from San Francisco, the highway rolls over brown hills, through apple orchards and sudden dark forests, then turns west, down into a valley full of sun.

It tops a headland and—behold—there's the sea! The Pacific glints like mica. Around a bend, pines pose a deep green asterisk against the sky. A scent of iodine is carried on the sea wind.

Elk, Prairie Creek.

12

*Stagecoaches on plank road in
the redwoods, between Fort
Bragg and Willits, in the 1880's.*

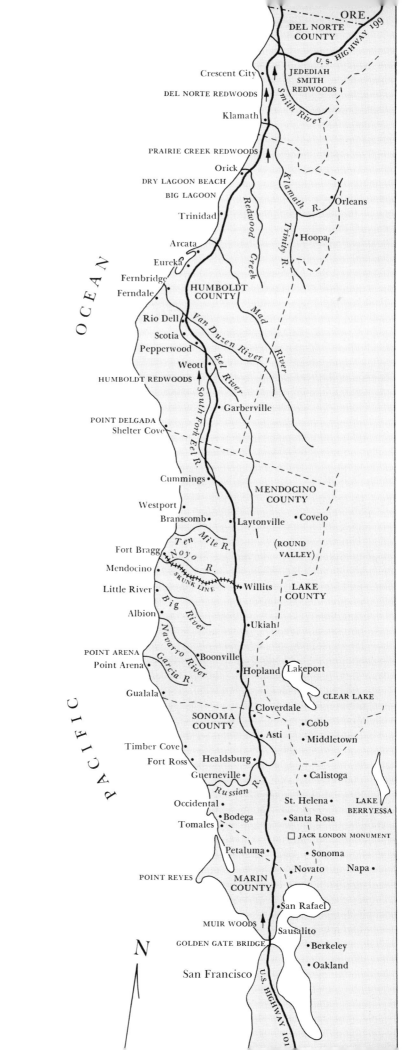

ORE.

DEL NORTE
COUNTY

U. S. HIGHWAY 199

Crescent City

JEDEDIAH
SMITH
REDWOODS

DEL NORTE REDWOODS

Smith River

Klamath

PRAIRIE CREEK REDWOODS

Orick

Klamath R.

Orleans

DRY LAGOON BEACH

Redwood Creek

BIG LAGOON

Trinity R.

Trinidad

Hoopa

Arcata

Eureka

Fernbridge

HUMBOLDT
COUNTY

Mad River

Ferndale

Van Duzen River

Rio Dell

Scotia

Eel River

Pepperwood

Weott

HUMBOLDT REDWOODS

South Fork Eel R.

Garberville

POINT DELGADA
Shelter Cove

Cummings

MENDOCINO
COUNTY

Westport

Covelo

Branscomb

Laytonville

Ten Mile R.

(ROUND
VALLEY)

Noyo

Fort Bragg

R.

Mendocino

SKUNK LINE

Willits

LAKE
COUNTY

Little River

Big River

Albion

Ukiah

Navarro River

Boonville

POINT ARENA

Garcia R.

Point Arena

Hopland

Lakeport

Gualala

CLEAR LAKE

Cloverdale

SONOMA
COUNTY

Cobb

Asti

Middletown

Timber Cove

Healdsburg

Fort Ross

Guerneville

Calistoga

Russian R.

Occidental

St. Helena

LAKE
BERRYESSA

Bodega

Santa Rosa

Tomales

□ JACK LONDON MONUMENT

Petaluma

Sonoma

Novato

Napa

POINT REYES

MARIN
COUNTY

San Rafael

MUIR WOODS

Sausalito

GOLDEN GATE BRIDGE

Berkeley

Oakland

San Francisco

U. S. HIGHWAY 101

OCEAN

PACIFIC

N

The eye picks out gray sheep grazing beside lichened wood fences, a salt-scoured barn, a fresh-cut woodlot, a bobbing fish boat. Senses sharpen and the spirit lifts.

To the east, coated grapes, hanging heavy from delicate vines, ripen in rows. Behind stone arches ancient arts are pursued, and the traveler is invited to sample the coolness and tart scents within. A warm breeze ruffles a deep-set lake beyond the vineyard.

Inside the forest, the floor underfoot is springy, deep. Sword fern and sorrel clover rim a faint path. Brush is sparse and no birds chirp. Few of the sun's rays can pierce this gloom. Immense rough columns rise a hundred feet and more before they branch out. Beneath the towering limbs lesser trees struggle. It is like some medieval court where knights pay homage to their lord.

Silent, cloaked in dignity for twenty centuries, the redwoods suggest a power beyond history. They merge past and present in their ancient trunks. Living entities, they are neither monuments nor mere trees. This one sprouted before Alexander humbled Persia. That one grew while Paul preached. They tower—in their pride of ancestry—the thousandth lineal descendants of botanic marvels that looked down on dinosaurs.

This eternal quality of the redwoods stuns mortals. Standing in the groves north of the Golden Gate, men feel linked at one great bound with prehistory and the limitless tomorrow. Questions come to mind: of mortality and man's relation to the universe.

Can humans learn wisdom from these trees? Perhaps—if they trouble to understand the redwood region, its history, and its relation to nature. From San Francisco Bay to Oregon, the empire that took its name from the tall trees offers much more than timber. Its strength can sustain the bursting West of America.

The towering trees are the preeminent attraction of the Redwood Empire, but the region is so vast and varied that many other facets claim attention. For easier comprehension it helps to split the region into its half-dozen natural compartments:

THE NORTH BAY: from the Golden Gate to Bodega Bay on the west, and through Sausalito to Sonoma and Santa Rosa on the east.

THE WINE VALLEYS AND LAKES: Napa Valley and its vineyards; man-made Lake Berryessa; mountain-girdled Clear Lake.

THE SOUTH COAST: From the Russian River north to the rugged hills of Humboldt. Some consider it the finest stretch of coastline in America.

THE INTERIOR WILDERNESS: Land of cattle wars, Indians, hunters, fishermen. Watershed of three turbulent rivers: the Klamath, the Trinity, and the Eel.

THE REDWOOD FORESTS: Golconda in timber. In 1964 the three tallest living things were found here.

THE NORTH COAST: From Eureka up to Oregon. Storm-crossed and forbidding since the days of the Manila galleons.

To discover this redwood kingdom takes one short trip; to know it well would take many lifetimes. Section by section, this is only an introduction.

*Lofty Coast redwoods dwarf passenger automobile
on Highway 101 in southern Humboldt County,
south of Pepperwood. More than two million
vacationing motorists each year visit
the redwoods in this spectacular roadside
forest.*

Redwood Empire

Beginnings: The North Bay

To Gaspar de Portolá, eighteenth-century Spanish governor of Lower California, the great swift strait leading into the bay was an impassable barrier. To Spanish mariners, and later, to clipper captains sailing around Cape Horn to reach the gold fields, its racing tides led to the greatest harbor ever seen.

John Charles Frémont, soldier-explorer, called the strait *Chrysopylae,* the Golden Gate. No poet since has improved on his inspiration, and Golden Gate it has remained.

This is the beginning of the Redwood Empire, the south portal. Here the pavement stops and rolling hills begin. North of *Chrysopylae* is a new land.

To the left lies Point Bonita. On the horizon, Mount Tamalpais, named for a sleeping maiden of Indian legend. To the right, off-lens, the vaulting bridge that links the metropolis to the Land of Big Hole in the Sky.

Golden Gate and Marin Hills.

Francis Drake, First Sojourner

Once pastureland, now suburbs—this is the familiar history of the counties north of the Bay. They dance to San Francisco's piping.

Marin and Sonoma would prefer to rule their own destiny, for they claim as proud a heritage as San Francisco's. In all, seven flags have flown here.

First came the White Ensign of England. It flew from the mast of that vengeful privateer, Francis Drake. Thirsting for a crack at Spain's riches in the Indies, Drake cleared Plymouth Harbor for Cape Horn in 1577, embarking on a round-the-world program of loot now, explain later. With a single ship, *Golden Hind,* Drake seized the Spanish galleon *Cacafuego* off Panama, thereby liberating enough silver to load his bark to her waterline. From Panama he sailed north into seas no Englishman had dared. *Golden Hind* was foul and leaky, and Drake needed a sheltered bay in which to careen her, caulk her seams, and scrape her clean.

In "stynkynge fogges" the English tacked blindly past the Golden Gate. A few miles northwestward, on June 17, 1579, the safe haven was found. Chaplain Francis Fletcher, whose chronicle alone has survived, recounts that in 38 degrees of latitude, the captain spied a "convenient and fit harborough."

There Drake lightened the ship of her treasure, tipped her sideways on the sand, and built a hasty stone fort under the bluffs. Fletcher says Drake named the land "New Albion" because the white cliffs reminded him of those near Dover.

Humble savages greeted the armored Britons as gods; their chief crowned Drake with a cap of feathers. The party took a few cautious steps inland, finding fat-cheeked ground squirrels and a milder climate. As July neared its close and the careenage was finished, Drake prepared to chance the uncharted Pacific, as Magellan had done. Off past the Farallones he sailed, pausing to snare a few sea lions for provender. The Indians burned signal fires in farewell.

Drake's dusky hosts kept no record of his visit, written or in legend. Maps of the voyage are vague and confusing when they depict California. How then can we fix the site of his careenage, which occurred a generation before Englishmen settled on the Atlantic Coast?

Fletcher's account of the voyage specifies that Drake left behind something solid and identifiable, a brass plate nailed to a stout redwood post. Engraved on the brass were bold words with which he took "possession of this kingdome whose king and people freely resigne their right and title in the whole land unto her Majesties keepeing."

Mindful of proud Gloriana's temper, her servant was also mindful to extend her domains wherever possible. This claim would perhaps augment his share of the loot. . . .

California historians for years tried to pinpoint Drake's secret harbor. They worked in the dark, because Drake delivered his logs and diaries to Elizabeth when he reached home, and Tudor archivists filed

Drake's "plate of brasse" by which he laid claim to California for the English crown. Hole at lower right was chiseled to hold an Elizabethan sixpence, not found with the historic treasure. Plate measures roughly five inches by eight inches, is a half-inch thick. It reportedly was first found near Drake's Bay in 1933, tossed away as worthless, rediscovered near San Quentin on San Francisco Bay three years later.

"The King of California places his Crown of Feathers on Admiral Drake's head." Engraving from A Curious Collection of Voyages, *printed in 1761.*

Sir Francis Drake, from a contemporary engraving, made about 1583. This would have been three years after he completed England's first circumnavigation of the globe four years after he became the first European to land on the California Coast. In 1588, Drake led the ferocious attack that smashed the Spanish Armada. He died in the West Indies in 1596, still fighting Spaniards.

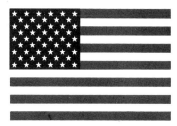

U.S.A. Since 1846

Bear Flag

Republic of Mexico

Mexican Empire

Imperial Russia

England

Seven flags have flown over Sonoma County

Spain

them so deep they have never come to light. Drake's Bay, under the lee of Point Reyes, seemed to fit Fletcher's description, but some scholars held out for San Francisco Bay itself.

Then in 1936 Drake's "plate of brass" was found. Near Drake's Bay three years earlier a passerby had picked it up, then tossed it away where another man rediscovered it. Authenticated, the precious relic now rests in the Bancroft Library at Berkeley.

To some buffs this is still inconclusive. But to the Drake Navigators Guild, formerly headed by the late Fleet Admiral Chester Nimitz, the lost careenage has to be The Estero, a shallow inlet at the top of Drake's Bay. They support their thesis with old maps, tide studies, and educated detective work on what sixteenth-century navigators might be expected to do. Final resolution of the mystery awaits further discoveries; meanwhile the public accepts Drake's Estero.

Drake's 40-day sojourn on the Redwood Coast was a dramatic chapter, but it had little lasting impact. Three centuries later Britain used his reports as a basis for territorial claims in Northwest America. Yet she gained only what she already occupied in Canada.

It remained for twentieth-century freebooters to reap the richest harvest. In 1936, eight men were tried in Chicago on mail-fraud charges. It was said they had persuaded thousands of Middle Westerners that they were heirs of Sir Francis Drake, and that—for a fee—they might gain great tracts in California, estates that were Drake's by right of discovery.

The swindlers were convicted, but Drake's phantom heirs were out $1,300,000, almost equal to the treasure their "ancestor" took off Panama.

Not for treasure but for clams, the late Fleet Admiral Chester Nimitz digs in The Estero. He was honorary chief of the Drake Navigators Guild, whose members continually research the great captain's visit to the California Coast in 1579. Currently a group of scientists armed with exotic electronic gear is sifting the sands of Drake's Bay for additional evidence.

Coast Redwoods, ferns, roots of a downed log in natural relationship beside Bull Creek in Rockefeller Redwoods State Park south of Eureka.

*White clay cliffs west of Drake's Estero
are identical when viewed from the sea to those
on the English Channel near Dover. Drake's
chaplain noted his master was struck by the
similarity and that it influenced him to
name his discovery "New Albion."*

The Original Settlers

For uncounted ages, the dwellers on the land were Indians, Coast Miwoks, a gentle people who believed the world was created by the Coyote God.

They lived in huts made from slabs of redwood bark, or of willow sticks thatched with reeds and plastered with mud. Naked, they hunted deer, gathered clams, in famine season munched on acorns and grasshoppers. Their diversion was a sort of sauna, or sweathouse. Into it the males dived, night and morning, for medicine and ceremony and also—in the winter—to keep warm.

They practiced social responsibility: at seasons when the red tide of Pacific plankton turned shellfish deadly poisonous, the Miwok posted guards along the beaches to warn less knowledgeable tribes away.

The Miwok lived at peace with their neighbors to the north, the Pomo and the Wappo, whose life cycle was equally uncomplicated. They had no written language, but a rich fabric of legend and superstition. Certain Indians, they knew, had the power to change their enemies into owls and bears.

A grimmer change was wrought by the first Spanish explorers. Missionary priests like Junípero Serra or José Altimira regarded the pagans as potential converts to the Cross. But the frontier overlords looked on them as cheap labor, docile, and easy to exploit. When the Indians resisted exploitation, their new masters exterminated them like rabbits. What the lash and the musket spared, alien smallpox took. From his tribe of 40,000 Suisuns, only Chief Solano survived. He had been tamed by the Spaniards.

Chief Olompali, last ruler of the Miwok, counseled friendship with the invaders. His son Ynitia therefore was granted 10,000 acres north of Novato, the only native to receive such largesse. But the reward was Ynitia's undoing: he sold out to an American for $5,200 in gold coin, then buried it. In 1852 someone slew the overprudent savage while trying to rob him. Ynitia's gold has never been found, and the Miwok are no more.

An old Pomo, 1931.

Pomo Indian Rancheria at Big River, Mendocino
County, about 1863. Discarded lengths of redwood from
a local sawmill are used to manufacture wickiups.

"Vaquero and Indian"—English writer-artist Frederick Marryat sketched sturdy
José Ramón Carrillo, General Vallejo's brother-in-law, during a visit
to Santa Rosa. It was Carrillo's pastime to hunt bears with a knife.

Spain Takes Hold

Delicate Ming porcelain now and then turns up in the Indian mounds on Point Reyes. These fragments almost certainly are part of the cargo of a Manila galleon, the *San Augustin*, wrecked by her willful master Sebastian Cermeno on the cape one gusty night in 1595.

Cermeno was the first Spaniard ashore, the first European after Drake. Warily and at long intervals, other servants of Spain peered at this hostile coast.

In 1775, following reports of the Portola expedition, a Spanish caravel finally crept into San Francisco Bay. Two months later Lieutenant Juan Francisco de la Bodega y Cuadra set a cautious foot on the sand north of Tomales Bay and unfurled the banner of Aragon and Castile.

Next year the Spanish broke ground for a mission church, a military Presidio, and a pueblo at Yerba Buena, later called San Francisco. At the Presidio there were questions about the northern lands: were they actually islands, as hinted by Lieutenant Bodega? Captain Quiroz, of His Most Catholic Majesty's vessel *San Carlos,* set out in a ship's boat to explore the upper bay. The first white man to penetrate the North Bay plain, he ascended Petaluma Creek as far as the modern town of that name.

Then ensued four decades of *mañana*. Indian converts were plentiful at Mission Dolores, in San Francisco, but they didn't thrive. The climate was chilly, the soil infertile, and bronchial complaints prevalent. Mission authorities deputed Fray Luis Gil Taboada in 1817 to establish a convalescent branch in warmer airs across the Golden Gate.

Taking his company of sickly neophytes, the friar found a proper site in a sheltered valley near the foot of a steep hill. Beyond lay unknown terrors, but Father Gil Taboada wrote Governor Sola: "I am willing to sacrifice myself in the service of these poor Indians."

Land was cleared for maize, an orchard, vineyards. A chapel and living quarters were raised from adobe brick. Word went out for new converts, and the curious Indians trooped in from Point Reyes and the northern rancherias. So successful was their conversion that they never returned to the hunt, the old rituals, and the sweathouse. Busy Mission San Rafael Arcangel soon was granted full status.

Mexico in 1822 declared herself independent of Spain, and a new tricolor flag flew from the missions, paying homage to the mad Mexican Emperor Iturbide. Conquest languished under the ramshackle empire, but the padres' push north was not yet checked. In mid-1823, zealous young Fray José Altimira led a party of exploration out of San Rafael. He had no liking for San Francisco as a mission site, and he wanted a new one to replace it. "An abundance of streams and springs, of wood and stone suitable for building" drew Altimira to where the present town of Sonoma stands. There he supervised construction of California's twenty-first and last mission—San Francisco de Solano.

Altimira's zeal was dampened by overbearing superiors, and his mission never did replace San Francisco. The conquistador spirit reappeared at Sonoma, where lonely soldiers turned to chasing the Indian girls. Vigor of another sort was restored in 1833 when Governor José Figueroa dispatched a remarkable *intendant,* Lieutenant Mariano Guadalupe Vallejo, to quell Indian raids and block the Russians, who had established a fur-poaching base on the Coast.

It remained for Vallejo to play out the final act in the drama of mission civilization. In 1834, the Mexican Republic decreed that all mission properties would be seized by the civil power. It was a death blow to San Rafael, Sonoma, and the other missions. The padres were sent home, their chapels became warehouses, and the Indian converts—unable to farm and no longer skilled in the arts of pagan life—drifted off and starved.

From the ruins flowered an exotic land-grant economy. A succession of Mexican governors gave away enormous tracts to cronies and relatives. The entire County of Marin, 521 square miles, was at this time owned by 23 persons. John Reed, an Irish seafarer, got the Tiburon Peninsula. Don Timoteo Murphy,

*Mission San Rafael Arcangel in downtown San Rafael,
reconstructed in 1949 to original plans. In 1829, 2,000 backslid
Indians raided the mission to "liberate" 200 converts. After
secularization in 1834, the adobe building sank into decay,
finally disappeared altogether about the time of the Civil War.
Some of its timbers were used to repair local streets.*

towering Indian agent, received Rancho Santa Margarita Las Gallinas y San Pedro, 21,679 acres north of San Rafael. Port Captain William A. Richardson's lands extended from the Golden Gate to Mount Tamalpais.

Biggest beneficiary of all was Henry Halleck, San Francisco lawyer who came to California as an Army officer during the Mexican War. He picked up 57,000 acres in Nicasio Valley when a friendly U.S. commission reviewed some Mexican grants in his favor.

Halleck went East to become a Union general during the Civil War. After some inconclusive battles, he earned the derisive nickname of "Old Brains." Perhaps he picked the wrong profession. Certainly there was nothing wrong with his wits in California.

Lord Charlie, Exurbanite

Mañana life on the big Spanish land grants ended soon after the Gold Rush. Small farms, often settled by squatters without benefit of title, became the rule. Once established, the belligerent squatters would resort to firearms rather than move.

The first of the more elegant settlers to come was Charles Snowden Fairfax, scion of Scottish and Virginian aristocrats. "Lord Charlie" was an early gold-seeker who had served as Speaker of the California Assembly. In 1856 he bought 40 acres and built a comfortable home in the town that now bears his name.

Two of hospitable "Lord" Fairfax's guests—state legislators—lent a back-to-the-frontier note in 1861. At odds over the Civil War, they fought a duel with rifles at Fairfax Manor. Dan Showalter left his opponent Charles Piercy dead on the lawn of honor.

After this encounter the lordly Charlie, a Southern sympathizer in a Union state, found his fortunes waning. He moved to Baltimore where he died six years later.

Improved ferry and rail service drew the first commuters to Marin County before the end of the century. Then after the 1906 earthquake wealthy refugees from San Francisco discovered Marin. In due time they took root in the redwood groves around Mill Valley and Ross. Their social life was active, refined, centered on tennis clubs and family entertainments. They looked with small favor on urban holidaymakers and picknickers whose new auto-mobility brought them by ferry across the Golden Gate.

Construction of the Golden Gate Bridge, in 1937, and Sausalito's shipyard boom during World War II erased Marin's splendid isolation. Gone was the four-month summer, the shaded tea parties. Homes for the newly rich sprang up on hillside and pasture, beside lagoons manufactured for boat-owners.

As the county closest to San Francisco, Marin was the first to experience postwar change. In the 1930's, Marin's population stayed manageable at around 40,000. Today it tops 192,000, and this is expected to double, and double again.

Lord Charlie wouldn't recognize the old place.

San Rafael in the early 1900's. Fourth Street, looking east from C Street.

Especially aquatic is Sausalito, "little willow" of the Spanish. Cascading down its steep hillsides are sun-decked villas, ancient hotels, artists' shacks, boxy apartments. There's also a modest San Simeon built on the foundations of a mansion that once housed young William Randolph Hearst. It has to be entered from above, by elevator.

Down on Bridgeway is a jumble of antique shops, art galleries, bars, over-the-water restaurants. A ferryboat houses a gift store. The bank or the post office exhibits "Pop" paintings. Beards and black stockings flourish. Tourists gawk.

At night Sausalito comes alive. Martinis and wine flow on various levels. Flamenco guitars and bongo drums throb. A paddle-wheel ferry welcomes nightclubbers. A former madam queens it in her café while silk-suited customers on expense accounts vie for a name to drop.

Outside the lights of Sausalito dance on the Bay. Afar, like Camelot, San Francisco rises into the night.

These commuters at Tiburon left San Francisco 35 minutes earlier by launch. Ferry is the last still operating on San Francisco Bay. Its more famous, much larger, ancestors quit in 1957, put out of business by various bridges. Now traffic jams are spurring a modest revival of this pleasant mode of travel.

Two of Sausalito's better-known characters in a rare togetherness pose: Sally Stanford (right), and Juanita Musson, with pet turkey. Sally reputedly was San Francisco's premiere bordello-boss, now owns the Valhalla, a Victorian-style eatery. Juanita's Galley, now closed by tax-gatherers, was known as a bistro where you got your eggs in your lap if you displeased the hostess. Irked by smug officialdom, Sally has twice tried for election to Sausalito's City Council. Despite backers who carried voters to the polls in a Rolls-Royce, she failed both times.

33

Artists and families in search of low rents
and aquatic living inhabit these arks at Sausalito,
despite periodic forays by the local health authorities.
Some of the derelicts have been burned to discourage tenantry.

Yacht Albatros *at anchor in foggy twilight off Sausalito.*

How William Kent Saved the Redwoods

One of the new barons of Marin County was William Kent, who moved west in 1871. His family had been Chicago meat-packers.

In 1903 a friend told Kent that a 300-acre redwood grove west of Mill Valley was about to be leveled by loggers. Kent borrowed $45,000 and bought the forest. It was better to lose the money than the trees, he told his wife.

A water company started condemnation proceedings, aiming to dam Redwood Creek and drown the redwoods. Kent countered this move by donating the grove to the United States. Red tape blocked acceptance, but Kent enlisted aid from John Muir, America's most famous naturalist, and from President Theodore Roosevelt, an ardent outdoorsman.

In 1908 Muir Woods—Kent insisted it be called that—became a national monument. At first there were no government funds to care for Muir Woods, so Kent paid for the upkeep of the road into the woods. Soon afterward he was elected to Congress, and while there helped create the National Park Service.

Despite his modesty, Muir Woods are William Kent's monument. To foreigners, his gift is a surprising chapter in our history. To the half-million yearly visitors who take the 45-minute ride from San Francisco, Muir Woods are not only a famous sight but an experience of serenity as well.

Enshrined between giant redwoods, bronze tablet commemorates a meeting of United Nations delegates at Muir Woods in 1945.

Keepers of the Flame

Point Reyes and Muir Woods are in Marin County by nature's gift, but their preservation is no accident. Marin people are powerful nature-lovers.

There are traces of New England in the county's approach to such matters. Congressman Kent's father was a Yale lawyer. Many of the settlers who fled San Francisco in 1906 were New Englanders, students of Emerson, Longfellow, and Lowell. In its formative years, Marin County had a closed, Back Bay air with Bostonian emphasis on rectitude in money management, and on admiration of the simple beauties of nature.

In Marin's natural setting there is much to admire: the quiet paths in Muir Woods, the Bishop pines of Point Reyes. Dominant Mount Tamalpais—"bay mountain" to the Miwok—is endowed with the Bay area's best hiking trails, and has an outdoor amphitheater. On the sea side, the sights range from the graceful crescent of Stinson Beach to the quaint oyster port of Bolinas, with a wildfowl sanctuary in the lagoon. West of San Rafael, San Geronimo Valley terminates in another redwood park, Samuel Taylor, on Papermill Creek. Along the shallow shoreline of Tomales Bay at Marshall there is an old wireless station. At sheltered Inverness, a former Czech minister of state runs an inn.

Intellectual pursuits became fashionable earlier in Marin than in most other Bay suburbs. Little theater movements and music festivals thrive. The county fair is mainly an art show. Shakespeare is popular beneath the Ross redwoods. Kafka and Rilke and "nonrep" art make the grade at Sausalito.

There are also the usual PTA and school board alarms about ticky-tacky subdivisions. But life's suburban pace is still leisurely in Marin, harking back to those 23 land grants and the Back Bay lawyers.

Congressman William Kent (center) *plays host to bearded John Muir and Secretary of the Interior Gifford Pinchot at Muir Woods Inn, terminus of the Mount Tamalpais & Muir Woods Railway. Railroad operated gravity cars into the forest, an 1,800-foot drop off Mount Tamalpais, from 1907 to 1930.*

Cape of Kings

Punto de los Reyes, Cape of Kings—so Sebastián Vizcaíno named the great bill-hook when he sighted it on the feast day of the Three Kings of the Epiphany. It is a regal landmass, or a queenly one. Francis Drake, in fact, gave it to Elizabeth I of England 24 years earlier, in 1579.

Whatever the royal precedence, Point Reyes assumes new importance today as a public preserve within sight of San Francisco.

It is the nation's newest national seashore. Full public use won't come until expensive acquisition processes are complete. A subdivision must be purchased from householders, and roads must be built. Ranchers who owned the cape for a century retain use of its windswept interior pastures. To date, only a few small strips provide public access to the water.

But pebble by pebble, the National Park Service is buying Point Reyes' beaches. Not for swimming: the water is too cold, and the undertow too perilous, but for hiking, for beachcombing, and for bird-watching . . . these are the gentle pleasures to be pursued on the Cape of Kings.

Point Reyes, air view to the northeast. Lighthouse occupies rocky tip, lower left; beach stretches 10 miles above it. In center distance, Drake's Estero.

Wright Is Wright

In Marin, postwar exurbanites confronted Back Bay old-timers reinforced by Portuguese dairymen, and the sparks flew. One such spark, which ignited a furious bonfire, was Frank Lloyd Wright.

The controversial architect was picked in 1957 to design a new county Civic Center on a 160-acre site north of San Rafael.

Wright was 88, dean of the "organic" school, which held that buildings should harmonize with their natural setting. He conceived the center as a series of arches between three knolls, and at a meeting in San Rafael he unveiled his plans.

Violent opposition developed over both the design and the cost—eventually more than $5,000,000. Wright meantime had extended his pronouncement to cover the swaybacked Richmond–San Rafael Bridge ("blow it up"), and Marin attitudes in general. He accepted the ensuing uproar as his due, intoning:

"Here is a crucial opportunity to open the eyes of not Marin County alone, but the entire country . . . to broaden and beautify human lives." Conservatives exploded.

As the storm raged, Wright died. His son-in-law and associates continued the job. But in 1960, a Supervisors' election turned on the Civic Center issue, the majority view changed, and in January, 1961, work was ordered halted while the Supervisors debated turning Wright's Byzantine palace into a hospital.

Now the New Spirit manifested itself in Marin, slicing across the old lines. Tract dwellers joined First Families to back the center. A newspaper poll found readers 7-1 in favor of continuing the work. It went forward again. The Supervisor who had led the anti-center forces was turned out of office.

Marin Civic Center's first phase, the Administration Building, spans hollow between hills north of San Rafael. At left, anodized-gold spire serves double duty as smokestack and radio antenna.

40

With Wright's widow as guest of honor, his center was dedicated in 1962. County workers grumbled they needed roller skates to get around, and there were hints that the plastic skylight leaked. But the blue, tan, and gold Civic Center is a traffic-stopper. Hundreds of tourists inspect it daily, ranking it in interest with Muir Woods. One guidebook calls San Rafael "chiefly interesting" for its Civic Center.

Wright's bold sketches project a fairgrounds, an auditorium, and a courthouse as future additions. Like the first Administration Building, these will be built on a pay-as-you-go basis.

The argument Wright began may never die. Nowadays Marin rather hopes it won't.

Architect Frank Lloyd Wright explains his drawings for Civic Center to Reporter George Wells at preview in San Rafael High School. Time was March, 1958.

Mount Tamalpais, fog veiling its 2,586-foot summit, can be appreciated from most homesites in Marin County. This view is from San Anselmo. Battlements of the San Francisco Theological Seminary lend a Bavarian touch.

Dillon Beach, on the north Marin coast.

Tomales Bay; oyster beds. Near here the old Marconi wireless station was converted in 1964 to headquarters for Synanon, the narcotic addicts' Alcoholics Anonymous.

43

Gringo! Andale! (Yankee, Go Home)

Mariano Guadalupe Vallejo, lieutenant in the Army of the Republic of Mexico, was just 25 when Governor Figueroa chose him to accomplish a triple task: pacify the Indians, block Russian colonial expansion, and take over mission properties north of the Bay.

Vallejo set out from Monterey in 1833 to carry feudal civilization to the Sonoma frontier. As *commandante-general* his powers were limitless. He settled his own family and that of his in-laws, the Carrillos, on land grants which cowboys measured by dragging a leather lariat along the ground. East of where Petaluma now stands, Vallejo built a huge adobe (mud-brick) fortress, laid out a broad plaza at Sonoma, and erected another adobe fortress there with a three-story tower from which to oversee his dominion.

Vallejo outlasted the Russians at Fort Ross, seized control of the mission properties, and dispatched his younger brother, Salvador, to teach some rebel Indians a lesson. In one series of battles, Salvador smashed the Sotoyomi tribesmen, killing 800 and taking 300 prisoners without the loss of a man.

By the middle 1840's, Vallejo's baronial fortunes were at their zenith. His Petaluma rancho alone measured 15 square leagues (66,662 acres). From it he harvested 72,000 bushels of wheat and barley in a single year, and shipped 50,000 hides in one consignment.

Affairs in Mexican California were nearing a crisis. The new Eden was filling fast with Yankee immigrants, flocking west by wagon train and ship. Spurred by troubles in Texas, war was brewing between the United States and Mexico. Early in 1846, Governor José Castro summoned a *junta* in Monterey to consider seeking the protection of England or France.

The farsighted *intendente* of Sonoma raised his voice in protest. Why court slavery under European despots? Vallejo asked. Better for California to accept her destiny, annex herself to the United States, "prepare for the glorious change . . . become not subjects, but fellow citizens."

This "most distinguished Californian" Mariano Vallejo assumed leadership of the pro-American party; Governor Castro led the anti-Americans. For the moment, Castro prevailed. Forerunner of another era, Castro ordered: "Yankee, go home."

Captain Salvador Mundo Vallejo,
famous Indian fighter
and strong right arm of his brother,
the comandante-general.

The Plaza of Sonoma, flanked by buildings, about 1865.
At left: barracks where soldiers of the Mexican garrison were housed,
behind the flagpole. At this corner in 1846 was raised
the Bear Flag of the short-lived California Republic. Right of the
barracks is Mission San Francisco de Solano, built in 1823, with a steeple
added later. Both buildings stand today, though the mission is
almost entirely a reconstruction.

General Vallejo and his granddaughters,
probably in the 1880's. He fathered
16 children, adopted six more,
a propensity which gave rise to family mirth.

A General Is Flagged Down

By 1846, 10 percent of California's population was gringo. The American settlers and trappers saw a good thing in this forbidden land, and they decided to defy José Castro's edict.

Captain John C. Frémont was in California on one of his periodic mapping tours for the U.S. Topographic Engineers. Frémont provided encouragement and a rallying point for the frightened Yanks. The prospective victims determined to strike first.

And so in the dawn hours of June 14, *Commandante-general* Vallejo was awakened by war whoops outside his *Casa Grande.* He peered out on the Plaza, spied some 33 armed Americans. Most wore greasy buckskins, many evidently were drunk. It was the momentous Bear Flag Revolt.

Hospitable Vallejo opened his front door and invited the rebels inside. Wines and brandies "sparkled in the glasses." Soon, according to historian H. H. Bancroft, "the bottles had well-nigh vanquished the captors." But there were dissidents to this roseate truce. Vallejo was carted off to Sutter's Fort (Sacramento). There the friend of American annexation was held captive for six weeks, on the ground that he carried a Mexican commission.

On the Plaza, a flag for the California Republic replaced the green, white, and red banner of Mexico. The new flag was designed by William L. Todd, a nephew of Mrs. Abraham Lincoln. In one corner was a red star, copied after the Lone Star of the Texas Republic. Facing the star was Todd's freehand version of a grizzly bear. Irreverent frontiersmen suggested it looked more like a hog.

The Bear Flag waved aloft until news came on July 9 of the U.S. declaration of war against Mexico. Then the Bear was superseded by the Stars and Stripes, hoisted by a Navy officer, grandson of Paul Revere.

Fiftieth reunion of the survivors of the Bear Flag Revolt, photographed at Sonoma in 1896. Only a few of the original 33 actually are shown.

46

*Balcony of the Spanish Barracks at Sonoma,
costumed local girls and flags betokening
the annual Vintage Festival, late in September.*

Later years brought an aura of fame to the Bear Flaggers, and hundreds of contemporaries claimed a part in the June revolt. An ensuing incident, the looting of Vallejo's home, was unmentioned.

Vallejo's fortunes declined steadily. The Bear Flaggers had run off his cattle and left his crops to rot. The great Petaluma rancho was sold piecemeal, or stolen by squatters. The *Casa Grande* burned in 1869. Litigation over his 150,000 acres took a fortune, but, for the most part, generosity was Vallejo's undoing. He gave away ranches like frijoles. When one acquaintance, a minister, complained that Vallejo's gift of 160 acres had been lost through faulty land titles, the general gave him another parcel with the admonition: "Never mind, this is better."

One of his Carrillo brothers-in-law, dispossessed of his estates, was reduced to peddling tamales in the streets of Santa Rosa. He had once donated the property on which the Sonoma County courthouse now stands.

In glory's twilight, the general and his big family lived at *Lachryma Montis,* a Swiss cottage northwest of Sonoma. Honored but in debt, he retained the pride of his station. When a wealthy admirer offered him funds, just before his death in 1890, the Father of California courteously refused. He commented sadly:

"After the horse is out, they would lock the stable."

Dairy ranch near Petaluma.

Soil Is the Payoff

The rich, sticky soil of the Redwood Empire's North Bay plain first produced crops in abundance for the Vallejos, the Carrillos, and their contemporaries. By the middle 1930's, Sonoma ranked as one of the ten richest agricultural counties in the nation.

Petaluma for decades was recognized as "The Egg Basket of the World." A Canadian poultryman, Lyman C. Byce, who came to town in 1878, originated the industry. In 1913, another Petaluman, Walter Hogan, wrote the classic of his trade, *The Call of the Hen*—the title was said to have been suggested by Jack London's *The Call of the Wild*. Hogan's work starred his two-year-old White Plymouth Rock, "Lady

Fountain and driveway at "Lachryma Montis," home of Mariano Guadalupe Vallejo, near Sonoma. "Tear of the Mountain" was named for the many springs issuing from the rounded hills to its north. The home is now a state historical landmark, open to the public.

Show You," which won the world's egg-laying title by emitting 281 eggs in one year. When William Jennings Bryan came through Petaluma, the Great Commoner asked for a copy of Hogan's book.

The world's only chicken pharmacy, specializing in poultry prescriptions, was in the Egg City. In the years before and after World War II, airline pilots used to chart their courses over Petaluma by the glare of incubator lights where, in 1952, 600 million eggs were laid.

Today's taxes, together with the high costs of labor and feed, have stripped Petaluma of its title, once a source of fun for vaudeville comics. Where 7000 hatcheries flourished, farmers now look to subdivisions for their profits, and the Egg Basket is scattered all over the West.

Vallejo Adobe east of Petaluma, partially restored and now a
state historical monument. In this courtyard Vallejo's 200 Indian plowmen
and other servants gathered each morning to receive
their instructions for the day. The "fortress" was started in 1834,
had adobe walls 2½ feet thick, and was buttressed with great redwood timbers,
hauled down from the forests by oxen. Here Vallejo superintended the manufacture of
cloth, saddles, carpets, and other necessities. Though it was built to repel
Indian attacks, the tribes never dared assault the huge building.
It was thoroughly looted during the Bear Flag Revolt.

Count Haraszthy Founds an Industry

Two centuries ago Father Junípero Serra, founder of the missions, introduced wine-grape culture to California.

But Father Serra's successors understood their spiritul tasks better than viniculture. They insisted on irrigating the vines, and their California wines had little distinction. Mission Indians placed the grapes in an oxhide, trampled them, left them inside the oxhide to ferment.

Count Agoston Haraszthy changed all that when he came to Sonoma in 1857. Scion of vineyard owners in his native Hungary, Haraszthy thirsted to produce Tokay and fine Bordeaux on the dry uplands. Irrigation? Barbaric! sniffed the noble vintner.

Harvesttime at Buena Vista about 1870, by the eminent photographer Eadweard Muybridge. At left, Captain E. P. Cutter, vineyard superintendent. Chinese workmen got $8 a month plus board, whereas white men demanded $30.

Agoston Haraszthy's elegant Grecian mansion
at Buena Vista. Here he and his countess entertained lavishly
at a great Vintage Ball in 1864.

Count Agoston Haraszthy, father of
California viticulture. From a portrait
made by Bradley & Rulofsen of San Francisco.

*Champagne corking at Buena Vista in the 1870's, by Muybridge. Dignified
beard examining the bottle, right background, is B. Eugene Auger, officer of
the Buena Vista Vinicultural Society, which took over operations from Haraszthy.*

He imported cuttings from Europe, traveled abroad to bring home vinous secrets, and set out more than 300,000 vines at his Sonoma estate, Buena Vista. He introduced the Zinfandel grape to the tables of California and the nation. His talent and enthusiasm literally created a new industry in the state, for Haraszthy encouraged Charles Krug, Emil Dresel, and Jacob Gundlach to plant vineyards nearby.

"California can produce as noble and generous wine as any in Europe," Haraszthy declared. He decreed there would be "no vintage years" in the state, because its climate precluded *non*vintage years. And he advocated redwood vats to replace hard-to-get oak cooperage.

Time proved the count correct. Today the valleys of Napa and Sonoma decant America's first wines, and the state leads all others in wine production. From 50,000 gallons a year in 1850, California's wineries today market more than 200 million.

53

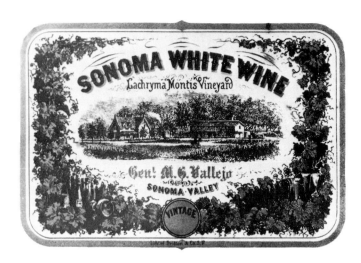

General Vallejo's famous Lachryma Montis label.

*Giant casks, imported from Europe,
line Buena Vista's cellars today.
Girl is in costume for annual
Valley of the Moon Vintage Festival at Sonoma.*

Agoston Haraszthy never lived to taste his triumphs. He was driven out of Buena Vista by speculators, including banker William C. Ralston, and migrated to the jungles of Nicaragua, where he was eaten by alligators.

Two miles east of Sonoma, Buena Vista lives on, the cradle of California viticulture. It lays claim to lost treasure: 30,000 bottles of Buena Vista champagne, buried somewhere in its stone tunnels by the 1906 earthquake. Legend has it that a Chinese caretaker was buried with the champagne, and that sometimes, when underground acoustics are just right, ghostly hiccups can be heard at Buena Vista.

54

Heartbreak House That Jack Built

Jack London, who lived like a meteor, left two burned-out shells in the Valley of the Moon.

One, the novelist's mortal ash, lies sealed forever beneath a red boulder in a grove of manzanita and redwood. The other, his dream castle "Wolf House" stands all bristling chimneys and rough stone arches, razed by an arsonist the night before London was to move in. On the west slope of this lovely valley Jack lived the last 11 of his 40 crowded years.

Up the valley through sleepy Glen Ellen, a sporting village which once supported 11 saloons, thousands of pilgrims come to share the memories. Jack London's vitality, compassion, and personal tragedy made him America's most widely read author.

"I am a sailor on horseback," he wrote. "Watch my dust!"

Some of that dust—London's rejection slips, his South Seas war clubs, his ancient dictaphone, his boxing gloves—coats the "House of Happy Walls," the cobblestone mansion his widow Charmian built after the writer's death in 1916. From Australia, from Russia, from Brazil, London worshipers come to stare at the relics in this National Historic Landmark. One Dane, stopping a day in San Francisco, taxied to Glen Ellen to lay flowers on his idol's grave.

Jack London, top American novelist at 30, takes his ease at his beloved "Beauty Ranch" in the Valley of the Moon.

Newsboy, oyster pirate, tramp, and Klondike miner before he was 23, London fell in love with the redwood slopes when he saw them in 1903 with Charmian Kittredge, soon to be his second wife. When *The Call of the Wild* became a runaway best seller, he took $7,000 of the proceeds and rushed to buy his first 129 acres.

At 30, Jack was the highest-paid author in America. *The Sea Wolf, Martin Eden, White Fang* and other novels brought him enormous royalties. Weary of roaming, he told poet George Sterling: "I am going to throw out an anchor so big and so heavy that all hell could never get it up again." In 15 years he was to write more than 50 books, and he plowed most of the proceeds into "Beauty Ranch," with the aim of creating the finest, the most *scientific* ranch-estate in the West.

More acres, concrete silos, stone piggeries, blooded Shire stallions—London bought them all in bursts of Londonian enthusiasm. He employed a hundred men, had a payroll touching $3,000 a month, entertained hoboes and celebrities around the clock. He spent $50,000 to plant 150,000 eucalyptus seedlings in an ill-fated attempt to market "Circassian Walnut," as the wood was then called.

Always used to writing 1,000 words a day, London had to increase his output and increase it again to meet the bills. He covered the Russo-Japanese War, the Vera Cruz Expedition, the Jeffries-Johnson prizefight. Still he outspent his income. Hospitable to a fault, Jack loaned hard-up pals more than $50,000 he never tried to collect. He even built a separate house (downwind?) for guests who didn't bathe.

Critical acclaim had come early to the brilliant young radical. London's raw realism reads unevenly today, but to contemporaries he was a sensation. He bridged the gap between Mark Twain and Hemingway. A world in revolt against the Old Order gasped at his portraits of the depths of society. As Lenin lay dying, his wife read him London's *Love of Life* and reported: "Ilyitch was greatly pleased."

For a lifelong Socialist, Jack entertained some contrary notions. "I write a book for no other reason than to add three or four hundred acres to my estate," he told an interviewer. He preached to the proletariat: "Wipe out private ownership of mines, mills, factories, railroads," but he didn't extend this category to ranches. "I'm going to stay right on my ranch at Glen Ellen and let the revolution go to blazes," he proclaimed one day. "I've done my part." Eventually he quit the Socialist Party, saying it had forgotten how to fight.

The former oyster pirate went from grandiose project to gilded scheme, climaxing his dreams of escape with the decision to build "Wolf House." It was to have 23 rooms, vaulted cellars, a fireplace in every room, a Roman bath. "It will last a thousand years," London exulted. He sank $80,000 and three years' work into the mansion.

The author as pig-tender. London built a concrete palace for his prize hogs at Glen Ellen, and visitors had to dip their shoes in disinfectant before entering. Less fastidious, the porkers developed pneumonia and ulcers from living on concrete.

Lonely stretch of Mendocino Coast north of Westport. Beyond the surf rises the dark and almost inaccessible King Range.

Picturesque Noyo, fishing village south of Fort Bragg.

Cottage on "Beauty Ranch" where London lived and died (in the glass porch). Though he spent fortunes building the ideal mansion, it burned before he could move in. This house lies outside public park boundaries and is not open to visitors.

Jack London, reinsman. Taken in 1911 when the author and his wife Charmian drove from Sonoma up the Coast to Oregon. This he captioned "Near Eureka."

In August, 1913, the magnificent house was ready. Jack and Charmian prepared to move from the cottage they occupied a mile away, up the slope. In the darkness, neighbors sounded the alarm: "Wolf House" was afire! Jack raced to the scene but the woodwork and the roof were ablaze in several places. Even lumber stacked outside was alight. As the night waned, Jack London's dream died hard. Nothing survived but the massive walls.

"We will rebuild," the fighter promised. But his creative impulses seemed to flag. Charmian's literary monologues (she called Jack "booful") affected his style to the point where London's female characters became painfully arch. He was accused of plagiarism, of nature-faking (Theodore Roosevelt scoffed when Jack wrote of a dog killing a lynx). London's years of writing under pressure drained him of ideas, and he was reduced to buying plots from young writers like Sinclair Lewis, who furnished *The Abysmal Brute*.

Prematurely aging, London felt his serious books were misunderstood. Muckraking had come into fashion, and the *New York World* criticized Jack's *Valley of the Moon* as a fairy tale. Only *John Barleycorn*, a saga of drunkenness, proved a sensation, and not in the way London intended. One critic wrote it betrayed the secret that booze was ruining Jack's talent.

Hurt, Jack threw himself more fiercely into battle, writing and managing "Beauty Ranch." In one last fine novel, *The Star Rover*, he compressed into brilliant episodes ideas originally intended for full-length books. Bouts of socializing down in Glen Ellen intensified. By 1915, London's tropical skin troubles and malaria (contracted on a voyage in his 45-foot yacht to the South Seas) were complicated by uremia, and he was frequently in pain. Opiates and rest were prescribed. But Jack scorned doctors and dined on raw fish, bourbon, and 12-minute duck. Trying desperately to find where he had failed his talent, he abused his friends and his iron constitution impartially.

On the sleepless night of November 21, 1916, London's "Noseless One"—death—came closer. Jack added an extra dose of pain-killer to his overburdened system. Doctors fought all next day to rouse him. Workmen shouted in vain that a favorite dam had burst. Jack died as the sun set behind "Beauty Ranch."

Glen Ellen mourned. No longer would his harness bells herald their hero's downhill dash to the 11 pubs, for a night of Olympian argument. The literary comet had fallen a victim to his own credo, emblazoned on the walls of his museum:

"The proper function of man is to live, not to exist. I shall not waste my days in trying to prolong them."

"Wolf House" takes shape on Jack London's 1,500-acre ranch a few weeks before it burned in 1913. "Finest house in America," the artist Harrison Fisher called it.

Ruins of "Wolf House" today—lava-rock arches and Roman plunge. "I pity the man who would do such a thing," London commented of the arsonist.

*Grown portly at 36, London surveys
the beginnings of "Wolf House."*

*Irving Shepard points to portrait of his uncle, Jack London,
aboard novelist's beloved yacht* The Snark, *in which he cruised
the South Seas. Son of London's older stepsister Eliza, Shepard
donated part of ranch property to state as memorial to the famous
writer. In foreground:* London's desk, chair, and dictaphone.

*Widowed in 1916, Charmian London built
"House of Happy Walls" near ruins of "Wolf House,"
filled it with memorabilia of her talented spouse.
Something of a recluse, she designed this porthole
in living-room wall to permit her
to peep at unwanted callers. She also built
hidden staircase leading from outside
to upstairs quarters. Charmian died in 1955.*

Was It Love at Fountain Grove?

It was a comely serpent that destroyed the Eden of the West, Thomas Lake Harris' exotic colony north of Santa Rosa.

The reptile was a lady—young Alzire Chevaillier, newspaper writer and suffragette. So devastating was Alzire's prose, printed in a San Francisco newspaper, that Mr. Harris fled his Brotherhood of New Life at Fountain Grove, its obedient disciples, its luxurious manor house, and its vintage wines.

According to Alzire's more purple passages, the bearded seer with the piercing eyes was running a harem for profit on the gentle hillsides. Readers of the 1890's ate it up.

Alzire employed an old journalistic dodge to gain entry into the select New Life Brotherhood. Chaperoned by her mother, she arrived at Fountain Grove in 1891, posing as a wealthy and eager postulant.

Harris fixed her with a hypnotic stare, advised her she would have to surrender her bank account to the brotherhood, and parked her in a communal dormitory to await spiritual indoctrination.

"You must wait for your heavenly bridegroom, Sir Knight Peace," Harris instructed the neophyte. "You will know when he descends from the celestial sphere, because you will feel it in your toes."

Meantime, she would receive a preparatory course from the Primate and King, as Harris called himself. But when Alzire called at his office to get the first lesson, she found her 68-year-old teacher with his feet in the lap of his shapely secretary, "Dovie Lee" Waring. The better to get his toes atingle?

Not so. The Primate and King explained he was assuming this position to facilitate "internal respiration," or New Breath, which descends from the Divine Spirit. Harris had visited heaven and hell several times, and he had inside information.

Miss Chevaillier continued skeptical. Later when Harris demanded a cash down payment on immortality, she packed up and went back to the city with Mama.

Soon San Franciscans were reading the lurid details. One of the expelled brethren was quoted as saying that Harris encouraged adultery at the colony under the name of spiritual marriage. A Swedenborgian minister declared that Harris had commanded one member to have relations with five women in one day.

Russian workmen built these storage barns at Fountain Grove winery, near Santa Rosa.

60

Thomas Lake Harris, founder and ruler of Fountain Grove. About 1875.

Fountain Grove. The mansion, today.

Harris, it seemed, used a simple and efficient system for controlling his disciples. Wives and husbands were separated, converts were separated from their money, and all further financial relationships were directed by the spiritual father—Harris.

The sage occasionally threw his brotherhood into ecstasy by describing his marriage with his celestial counterpart, Queen Lilly of the Conjugal Angels, who had borne him two children somewhere in Outer Space.

Two of Harris' most distinguished converts were British—Lady Oliphant and her son, Laurence. Laurence was married, but Harris refused to permit him to live with his wife until the latter had assigned her dowry to the brotherhood. The long-suffering nobleman at length broke with the Primate and King, sued and collected $90,000.

Fountain Grove, it turned out, was the culmination of several earlier Harris experiments in communal living, breathing, and fiduciary finance. A minister of various faiths, he had operated similar colonies in New York State. He also claimed friendship with the literary elite of the day, including Horace Greeley, Nathaniel Hawthorne, and Edgar Allan Poe.

"America's best-known mystic," the erudite William James called him. And Lady Byron said she liked to commune with her long-dead spouse through hearing Harris read his poetry, possibly *Don Juan*.

Finally the pressure became too great for the bearded Primate and King. He packed, married his footstool "Dovie Lee" and decamped with her to New York. There he embarked on his final celestial visit a few years later.

At Fountain Grove the faithful waited three months for Harris' promised resurrection. When this failed to take place, the Brotherhood of the New Life began to break up. Yet part of it was to endure in mellowed vintage at Santa Rosa for almost three decades.

Among Harris' disciples were several Japanese youths he had drawn from their studies in England. One of them was a talented and dignified nobleman, Kanaye Nagasawa. While Harris was dealing with the birds-and-bees side of Fountain Grove, Nagasawa was developing practical agriculture. So well did he direct the digging and planting that 400 of the estate's 1,500 acres were transformed into one of California's greatest vineyards. Winemaking became the mainstay of the colony after Harris left, and the Fountain Grove label was honored around the world.

Baron Nagasawa outlived his fellow colonists, dying in the great house in 1934, at the age of 83. The estate passed into other hands, the vineyards were rooted out, and the place is now a cattle ranch.

Was Fountain Grove actually a hotbed of free love? Testimony conflicts, and for every foe who proclaimed Thomas Lake Harris a swindling libertine, a defender arose to deny it.

Whatever his morals, the spiritualist with the burning eyes and the tingling toes left a spicy legacy to the Redwood Empire.

61

Plant Wizard of Santa Rosa

In pleasant Santa Rosa stands a living shrine to one of the world's most beloved naturalists, a self-taught genius with a green thumb.

Luther Burbank, who welcomed kings and presidents to his modest home opposite Juilliard Park, lies buried in his garden under a spreading deodar.

By the time of his death in 1926, Burbank had developed more than 800 varieties of fruits and flowers for the benefit of his fellowmen. The Burbank potato, spineless cactus, thornless blackberries, Shasta daisies—all grew from Burbank's meticulous experiments. It was customary for him to raise as many as 40,000 hybrids, select the best single specimen, and destroy all the others.

Giant spineless cactus thrives on grounds of Luther Burbank's home in Santa Rosa. Burbank developed species and it proved a valuable item of feed for cattle in desert areas. In rear: Burbank's carriage house.

62

Luther Burbank, the Santa Rosa hybridizer.
"No man knows anything that is final," he declared.
"Wait awhile. Hold your horses!"

A frail youth from Massachusetts, Burbank landed in Santa Rosa in 1875. He became a successful nurseryman, but finding that his experiments absorbed more and more of his attention, he closed his business in 1893 to devote full time to his tests, both at Santa Rosa and on a farm near Sebastopol.

His fame spread. Thomas Edison, Henry Ford, President Taft, Harvey Firestone, and King Albert of the Belgians were among those who came to Santa Rosa to see the man who called himself only "a good gardener." Though he could have patented his products and become a millionaire, Burbank chose not to do so, leaving them free for everyone to use. Among the wonders of his garden were an apple tree with 526 varieties in its branches, and a cherry tree with more than 400.

Of the Santa Rosa Valley, he wrote home to Massachusetts: "The climate is perfect, the air so sweet it is a pleasure to drink it in." His valley, Burbank often said, was the chosen spot of all on earth.

Burbank's widow still lives in the garden-home, now a public park. March 7, the plant wizard's birthday, is observed as California's Arbor Day, and he is revered as Santa Rosa's most illustrious citizen.

Wine Valleys and Lakes:
The Napa Valley

Close enough to San Francisco for a long commute, the drowsy vine-carpeted Napa Valley is being discovered anew. Slightly more distant, Lake Berryessa and Clear Lake appeal to active sports-lovers.

The scene north of Napa evokes memories of bygone vintners, of nabobs at race meets in their tallyhos. Old and new combine without conflict—the stone winery and the assembly line of corks and bottles. In Napa Valley, machinery hides behind weathered stone.

Vineyard near St. Helena.

Sam Brannan's Freudian Sip

Sam Brannan was a Mormon, but a merry one.

He arrived in San Francisco two years before the Gold Rush. By 1850 he was the new state's first millionaire.

Sam Brannan founded San Francisco's first newspaper, its fire department, its first Vigilance Committee, its first flour mill. When gold was discovered on the American River, he was the first into San Francisco with a bottle of nuggets. He owned a fifth of all the real estate in San Francisco, a quarter of Sacramento.

In short, he was an enterprising man. In 1859, with fortune smiling on Sam Brannan, he looked afield for new enterprises. A sleepy hot-springs resort north of Napa proffered opportunity. Here he determined to build a fashionable spa, the counterpart of New York's famed Saratoga.

His tongue tangled by the local product, Sam toasted in prophecy:

"It'll be the Calistoga of Sarafornia." And Calistoga it remained.

The pioneer promoter poured half a million into the Springs Grounds Hotel. He persuaded a railroad to extend its tracks to Calistoga. By the early 1860's he was deeply in debt, banking on the success of his huge resort.

Sam Brannan, Gold Rush plunger and founder of Calistoga,
surveys the California scene with Gaelic aplomb.
Seated are two contemporary California financiers, Thomas Larkin (left),
U.S. Consul at Monterey in the Mexican era;
and William D. M. Howard.

Last of the cottages at the Springs Grounds Hotel,
Calistoga, built by Sam Brannan in 1858.
In one of these Robert Louis Stevenson and his bride
stayed briefly awaiting cheaper quarters on the mountain.
Stevenson mentions the palm trees.

Legend alive. Clark Foss, Hercules of the
stagecoach fraternity, takes top-hatted
party from Calistoga to the geysers in 1880's.
Stevenson recounts his first telephone
conversation attempting to interview Foss.
His reward was a few grunts.

Fashion betrayed Sam Brannan. The elite of San Francisco, the Leland Stanfords and the Charley Crockers, withheld their patronage. Springs Grounds' coaches continued to greet incoming trains, but few nabobs climbed aboard.

In vain did Sam Brannan mortgage his land, in vain tempt local ranchers to try his silkworms and his Merino sheep. Peccadilloes with actresses like Lola Montez alienated Mrs. Brannan, who divorced him and took part of his wealth—a foretaste of California's community-property settlements. By 1875, Sam was broke.

Merry no more, Sam Brannan left the land he had once ruled, and died penniless in 1889. Not long ago a dispute flared between Calistoga and San Diego, the town where his remains lie. Calistoga wanted to reinter its first citizen's body in honored ground up north. San Diego refused.

Now each September, Calistoga tries to make it up to Sam Brannan by donning whiskers and crinolines, to spend three days and nights in dancing and toasting the Merry Mormon.

Treasure Island on Calistoga's Mountain

After six months of near-starvation in San Francisco, and near death from tuberculosis, author Robert Louis Stevenson arrived in Calistoga in May, 1880. He had just married Fannie Osborne—his senior by 11 years—and hoping to recover his health, he had brought her to Calistoga for their honeymoon. With them was Fannie's small son, Lloyd, and their dog, Chuchu. They stayed, rent-free, in a miner's rickety cabin.

A more ill-omened honeymoon cannot be imagined, but in the bracing air above Calistoga, on the shoulder of Mount St. Helena, the miracle happened. Stevenson's health improved, and after three months' stay, he was able to resume an active life. He died in the South Seas 14 years later.

No trace of Stevenson's honeymoon hovel remains. But the writer immortalized the place, and the valley below, in a series of charming sketches titled *Silverado Squatters,* which was published in London in 1884.

Interior of Robert Louis Stevenson's cabin near Calistoga, from a drawing by his brother-in-law, Joe Strong, to illustrate Silverado Squatters. *Wind blew unobstructed through the chinks, and poison oak sprouted through cracks in the floor, but Stevenson thought the "picnic" atmosphere just right for his honeymoon.*

The road to Silverado still exists above the modern highway. on the wooded side of Mount St. Helena. Shed is of later vintage than Stevenson's cabin, but of similar appearance.

Monument—an open book—marks site of Stevenson cabin, long since disintegrated. Visitors find it only after an arduous climb up from the highway.

"We are in a land of stage drivers and highwaymen," Stevenson wrote. "A few years ago the Lakeport stage was robbed a mile or two from Calistoga. In 1879 the dentist of Mendocino City suddenly threw off the garments of his trade . . . and flamed forth in his second dress as a captain of banditti." After a chase and much gunfighting, the dashing toothpuller "bit the dust." And Stevenson was "reminded of another highwayman of that same year. 'He had been unwell,' so ran his humorous defense, 'and the doctor told him to take something, so he took the express box.'"

Indeed it was not until 1900, when the first auto stages appeared, that the Calistoga & Clear Lake Stage Co. dispensed with guards and shotguns. Buck English, that "prince of highwaymen," of whom Stevenson wrote, was captured in 1895.

Drivers like Clark Foss, a 265-pound giant who ran tourists up to the geysers in northern Sonoma County, were folk heroes. "Along the unfenced, abominable mountain roads," Stevenson recounted, "he launches his team with small regard for human life or the doctrine of probabilities." Foss could handle six horses like so many cats, and was more of an attraction than the geyser. Eventually he paid the price for his daring. He was dragged to death.

Always more interested in people than places, Stevenson tells of "Petrified Charlie" Evans, a seafaring man who found the famous Petrified Forest west of Calistoga while clearing a field in 1871. And of Jacob Schram, itinerant barber and native of the Rhineland. His hillside vineyard produced the famous Schramberger vintages which found favor in London's finest clubs. Stevenson savors a wine tasting in Schram's cellars, "resting on pillars, like a bandit's cave." His host performed this "solemn office," and "followed every sip with a proud anxiety."

Local version of Old Faithful spouts on schedule at Calistoga, spurred no doubt by 75-cent admission charge for tourists. Calistoga still attracts rheumatism and arthritis sufferers who bake out their ills in its mud baths. Curative claims for Napa Valley spas produced such facilities at St. Helena Sanitarium, founded in 1878, now operated on a big scale by Seventh-Day Adventists.

Jackson's Napa Soda Springs, at the height of its fashion in the 1890's. The mineral waters attracted socialites and Bonanza kings from San Francisco. The resort offers only a few ruins today.

Mount St. Helena, rising above flowering orchards in
the Napa Valley. In 1840, this 4,344-foot peak was ascended
by a party of Russian naturalists from Fort Ross, who
placed a copper plate naming it for Princess Helena
Gagarin, wife of the Fort Ross manager. The plate later
was removed and lost in the San Francisco fire of 1906.
Legend says the beautiful blonde princess was the
object of a kidnap plot hatched by a giant Indian,
Chief Solano, while she and her spouse were visiting
General Vallejo at Sonoma. The general learned of the potential international
incident while the chief was in his cups, locked the
passionate redskin in the calabozo *until his ardor cooled.*

Stevenson, Fannie, and little Lloyd "squatted" through July in the breezy cabin. The author made notes on local people and customs, on the summer sea of fog which he observed from above, and on the starry nights and sunny days on Mount St. Helena. Their cabin at Silverado was once part of a prosperous mining camp. Cinnabar and then silver had been discovered here in 1860, and by 1874 the camp had a population of several hundred. By 1880, however, it had sunk into permanent decay. Stevenson explored the old mine shafts, reconstructing its past glory in passages prophetic of *Treasure Island*.

Today the site is a state park. A steep mile's walk discloses only a monument in the form of an open book, dedicated to Stevenson. On the right-hand page is a quotation from Stevenson's poem to the dead son of a friend, Fanny Sitwell, ending: "Came and stayed and went, nor ever ceased to smile."

Smashing Fun in the Valley

"Who prates of want or war after taking wine?"

Thus the poet Horace, and thus twenty centuries later, Napa Valley dwellers, and throngs of sipping visitors.

The first vines in the valley were planted by George Yount, buckskin rifleman who came west in 1831. Yount laid a split-redwood shingle roof on General Vallejo's great adobe fort at Petaluma, and the general rewarded him with two square leagues of land (around present-day Yountville), over the roofer's protest that this was too big to be manageable. But by 1860 Yount was managing to squeeze 5,000 gallons of wine a year from his land. Other pioneers got the urge to plant, and by 1870 Sam Brannan, for example, was distilling 90,000 gallons of brandy at Calistoga.

Charles Krug, native of Prussia, worked awhile for Count Haraszthy, then crushed grapes for the early experimenters in the Napa region, eschewing the mission-Indian oxhides. Finally in 1861 Krug established his own winery, which endures under his name.

Beringer Brothers, with cool cellars hewn out of the soapstone hills by Chinese labor, started winemaking in 1876. At St. Helena they built their Wagnerian "Rhine House" whose stained-glass glories include a memorable tasting-room.

Beaulieu Vineyards, founded in 1900 by George De Latour, and the vineyards of Louis M. Martini, just south of St. Helena, are notable establishments. The Christian Brothers, religious order, have a winery and novitiate eight miles northwest of Napa and an impressive stone cellar at St. Helena, which when William Bourn completed it as a cooperative in 1889 was said to be the world's largest.

Inglenook Winery, near Rutherford. Founded in 1879 by Captain Gustav Niebaum, a Finnish seafarer, it remained in his family until recently. Inglenook gallonage is small but its prestige is high.

The nabobs of the Comstock and the Central Pacific were early discoverers of the Napa Valley. It was considered very chic in the 1870's to own a vineyard and a private winery. Many of these survive, converted into châteaux by today's successors to the nabobery.

With them survives—especially after a few sips of Napa Burgundy or Chablis—a unique "feel" of California and its beginnings.

The wine business is burgeoning in the Napa and Sonoma valleys. The only difficulty is growing enough grapes, for there is only so much proven wine land, and even that is under constant threat from subdividers, pushing north with bulldozers.

Cellar and cooperage at Beringer Brothers Winery, near St. Helena. Some caves run 1,000 feet into the hillside.

Beringer Brothers employees celebrate repeal of Prohibition in 1933, hamming it up in front of their winery at St. Helena. The ban on potables destroyed many smaller wineries in California, but Beringer's hung on, sustained by legal loopholes, which allowed the firm to sell wine for religious purposes. There are four Beringers in this photo. Man at right holds fencing mask, used to protect face from exploding bottles while turning champagne.

73

*Wine grapes ready for crushing
at Charles Krug Vineyards, St. Helena.*

Wine on the table is respectable today. In America, 95 percent of all wine drunk is American; 90 percent of it comes from California. Authorities rate Napa Valley wines—the best, most carefully aged varieties—with the top 10 percent of Europe's exports. They may not equal the great years of the Côte d'Or, or Schloss Johannisberger, but they are well above the *vins ordinaires* and on a par with non-vintage years of French estate bottlings.

The premium producers, who own their own vineyards or buy from tested wine lands, lay increasing stress on quality. So they label their products with something equivalent to the European grape which tutored American palates: Pinot Chardonnay for Chablis or Pouilly-Fuissé; Sauvignon Blanc for dry Graves; Gamay Beaujolais for the light Burgundies. But this bow toward the Old Country is only the return of an ancient favor.

Haraszthy brought back 200,000 European cuttings in 1861. Thirty years later the phylloxera epidemic devastated Europe's vineyards. California had whipped phylloxera a decade before. So California shipped thousands of phylloxera-resistant cuttings back to their parent countries to help Europe reestablish her wine industry.

Thus the vineyards of Napa and Sonoma paid their debt—with interest. Today, distinctive and mature, they pursue their independent destiny.

74

Vineyard workers at Inglenook prune and train the vines each spring. Without this care, canes grow wild, harvest is uncertain.

Cultivating vineyard by horse and plow is a rare sight nowadays, but a few steep hillside acreages in the Napa Valley continue the practice out of necessity.

75

Part of the fun for visitors during harvest season is watching the ripe bunches dumped into the winery preparatory to crushing.

. . . and another important ceremony is wine tasting. Only a sip of each variety is offered, but there seems no practical limit on the amount of sips. This scene and the one above are at Charles Krug winery near St. Helena.

After bottling, wines are stored neck down to keep corks moist and air free. Roy Raymond, manager of Beringer Brothers, St. Helena, examines a special vintage in the firm's limestone cellars, hewn into the hills generations ago by Chinese labor.

Sunlight on the old winery door at Schramsberg. Here in 1880 honeymooner Robert Louis Stevenson sampled the proprietor's Golden Chasselas.

A gathering of notables at Asti, north
Sonoma County, in 1896 celebrates the visit
of Prince Luigi of Savoy, of Italy's royal
house, to Italian Swiss Colony vineyards.
Flanking the prince are Andrea Sbarboro
and Pietro Rossi, prime movers at Italian
Swiss, which Sbarboro founded in
1881 to provide jobs for unemployed
fellow-countrymen. Asti, 85 miles
north of San Francisco, on Highway
101, is the most-visited winery in the
Redwood Empire, hosting more than
300,000 sip-and-see tourists each year.

Shaped like a wine cask, Madonna
del Carmine Church at Asti
copies older chapel in distance.

At right, Arnold Ford's hop kiln near Ukiah,
caught in a late-nineteenth-century glass
plate by Photographer A. O. Carpenter. The
valley of the Russian River was California's
foremost hop-growing region for a century,
but rising costs and competition have
reduced plantings in Sonoma and Mendocino
counties to the vanishing point.

78

Wine had no monopoly on bottled cheer
in the Redwood Empire. Above is a twin-steepled oasthouse
near Sebastopol where hops were cured before
becoming malt for beer. Russian River
curves in distance. Orchard,
in bloom, has supplanted hops.

Andrea Sbarboro's fountain,
in the atrium of his Pompeiian villa at Asti.
Sbarboro loved practical jokes,
outfitted his estate with
hidden traps which squirted water
on unwitting guests.

Mountain Enclave

North of Napa, the Redwood Empire forgets the discothèques. Isolated by its rings of mountains, Clear Lake dozes quietly most of the year, a retreat for black bass and retired handymen. On Memorial Day, its 300 waterside resorts and marinas spring to life with a roar that lasts until after Labor Day. Yet Lake County remains a land of one-room schoolhouses and volunteer fire departments.

In the last century, the only access to the shallow, tadpole-shaped lake was over a Hobson's choice of 15 toll roads, some with grades approaching 35 degrees. (The last one of these, the road to Bartlett Springs, endured until 1923.) Indians clung to their primitive ways in Lake County longer than in most other parts of California—there are still about 400 Pomos around.

Two roughneck frontiersmen, Andrew Kelsey and Charley Stone, made a living by enslaving the simple Pomos in 1847–48. Cruelty was Stone's and Kelsey's undoing. A squaw they forced to live with them poured water down their gun barrels, and they were slain by the long-suffering tribesmen. In revenge, a party of soldiers under Captain Nathaniel Lyons struggled up from Benicia in 1850, lugging two longboats garnished with brass cannon. The amphibious expedition cornered more than 100 Indians at Bloody Island, south of the present town of Upper Lake, and massacred them all—men, women, and children. (Lyons paid later for his cruelty—at Wilson's Creek, Missouri. He was the first Union general to die in the Civil War.)

Lakeport in the 1870's, by A. O. Carpenter of Ukiah.
Mount Konocti dominates unsullied Clear Lake.
After a running battle with Lower Lake for the county seat,
Lakeport won the last election in 1870, promptly built
the courthouse (center) *which is still used today.*

Hereford bull lords it over Guenoc Ranch,
once owned by Actress Lily Langtry.
Only 100 miles from San Francisco,
southern Lake County is sharing
in the weekend-ranch boom
enjoyed by Napa and Sonoma counties.

Boat harbor, north side of Clear Lake.
Mount Konocti, in the distance,
is 4,200 feet high.

Bartlett pears and sulfur spas laid the foundation for Lake County's economy in the 1890's. Gnats all but ruined it later, the winged pests swarming thick enough to smother oil lanterns. Lake County officials in the 1950's and 1960's used insecticides to kill gnat larvae, and Rachel Carson complained they had poisoned the local birdlife. But recent reports indicate the program has controlled the gnats without diminishing Clear Lake's bronzeback bass. These fighters are sometimes dipped straight out of the tules with a 12-foot pole, a method developed by Clear Lake guides.

Celebrities add a fillip of interest to Lake County's pastures and piney ridges: Lily Langtry, Edward VII's favorite, once bought Guenoc Ranch, south of Middletown, intending to breed racehorses. The Jersey Lily gave up when a trainload of her thoroughbreds died in a train accident back East, and Guenoc's 23,000 acres recently were traded for 37 acres near Honolulu.

Jimmy Durante loved to summer at Lower Lake in the 1920's. TV Star Ernie Ford works 540 acres northeast of Clear Lake, in Long Valley. A truck labeled simply "E. J. Ford" takes Ole Ern's Herefords to market and fair; his foreman's name is on the mailbox.

Lake County is gaining favor as a leisurely, inexpensive place to retire. A recent census shows a quarter of its population of 15,000 is over 65, and 22 percent are on Social Security.

81

Retirement Bonanza

Retirement is big business these days. Mild climate and proximity to big cities have brought retirees by the thousands to the southern Redwood Empire.

The pleasant Valley of the Moon has enough admirals in drydock and colonels out to pasture to stock a senior-grade Pentagon.

First to colonize the area around Sonoma were Admiral and Mrs. Charles M. Cooke. Mrs. Cooke had met the Jack Londons in Honolulu before World War I, and after hearing Charmian London's description of Sonoma, she determined to build a retirement home there. When "Savvy" Cooke (Annapolis '10) brought his ship under the newly completed Golden Gate Bridge in 1937, the couple explored the hilltops around Sonoma, and finally bought a lofty crow's-nest east of town.

The most famous military family to settle here was the H. H. "Hap" Arnolds, who came up while the general was commanding the Army Air Corps during World War II. General Arnold made the Spreckels Ranch near Glen Ellen his home. The aviation strategy that brought Germany and Japan to their knees was formulated in the Moon Valley. "Hap" Arnold died at his home on Arnold Drive, and his collection of airplane models is on display in Sonoma's town hall.

Today the roster of retired military men in the valley includes Vice Admiral Thomas B. Williamson; Colonel Norris M. L'Abbe, a former cavalryman; and Colonel Arthur T. Brice, who operates a microphotography business from his home southeast of the Plaza.

"When we came here, we were the first service people," recalls Mrs. Cooke. "Now you can't throw a stick without hitting a colonel."

Admiral Cooke, adviser to Chiang Kai-shek in 1949–50, and before that commander of the Seventh Fleet and chief of staff for Fleet Admiral Ernest King, is a staunch patriot as well as staunch Sonoman. When Khrushchev visited America a few years ago, the admiral half-masted the colors at his ranch and kept them in mourning until the Red chairman went home.

Skiing behind a swift inboard,
Patti Love is mirrored in placid waters
of lower Clear Lake.
Ahead is 4,200-foot Mount Konocti,
hallowed in Indian legend,
and later called "Uncle Sam" by local
settlers because soldiers camped on its slopes.

Lake County has its piney woods too;
these are on the side of Cobb Mountain,
whose 3,000-foot elevation
gives vacationers respite from summer heat.
Family-style resorts and summer-home tracts flourish.

*Outboards race almost any
summer weekend opposite
Clear Lake Highlands.*

*At Lower Lake is the one-room
jail, built in 1878 and
much photographed.
Keen rivalry flourishes
among various resort
complexes around
Clear Lake.*

*Vacationers dip in the pools at
Hobergs, Forest Lake, or Seiglers Springs,
three of the most popular
Cobb Mountain resorts.*

*General of the Air Force
H. H. "Hap" Arnold donned Western regalia
in 1947 to help dedicate a monument
at Buena Vista winery.
The general retired to a Sonoma ranch
shortly after World War II.*

*Colonel Lawrence Clark, retired Army officer,
served as president of the Sonoma County Taxpayers'
Association. Colonel Clark lives near Santa Rosa
on six acres he bought for less
than a city-size lot would have cost him
on San Francisco's Peninsula.
He likes the region
for the climate and proximity
to Bay area PX's and military hospitals.*

*Admiral Charles M. Cooke,
wartime plans chief of the U.S. Navy,
brings his brass hat out of mothballs.
Dean of the retired-officer colony around Sonoma,
Admiral Cooke likes to recall
momentous days with Franklin D. Roosevelt
at Yalta, is a voluminous writer of
Letters to the Editor.*

*Joe Mazzola, business manager of the
Plumbers & Steamfitters Local 38,
surveys luxury pool
at union retirement-and-recreation center
on Clear Lake.
Plumbers' paradise is this
90-acre complex of apartments, marinas, and
recreation facilities at Konocti Harbor.
Estimated cost exceeds $8 million.*

Up in Lake County, there's a different sort of leisure colony, operated by Local 38, Plumbers & Steam-fitters Union, of San Francisco.

The local has more than 3,000 members. A few years back, a contract was negotiated for the majority of them, workers in the building trades, which provided that employers should pay about 10 cents an hour into a union retirement fund. Now grown to millions, the fund has been used to build a 90-acre plumbers' paradise at Clear Lake.

Joe Mazzola, business manager for the local, calls Konocti Harbor "my dream." Already it has 40 apartment units, a recreation hall and a 600-seat dining room, swimming pools, launching ramps, and marinas. Ultimately there will be 50 retirement homes for members, nestled against Mount Konocti; also a convalescent center for sick brethren.

"We had plenty of beefs before some of these people could understand it," confides Joe. "Now they realize there's nothing like it." Unity House, the garment workers' retirement complex in Pennsylvania's Poconos, is "for checker-players and shuffleboard players, compared to this," the union official continues.

Mazzola is reluctant to set a price on his dream. Local resort owners guess at something like $8 million to date. They also hint that the plumbing doesn't work.

But Mazzola & Co. are surfing on the crest of something like a half-million annual income. San Francisco's plumbers, who make around $7.50 an hour, clearly are the new aristocracy of enterprise, and Konocti Harbor is their Palm Beach.

The Drowned Valley

In postwar years, populous California's water became so precious that mankind had to give nature an assist in storing the stuff.

Runoffs had to be dammed-up for irrigation and flood control. This led to a most popular by-product—the new man-made recreation lakes springing up throughout the water-rich north coastal portion of the state.

One of the largest offspring of this marriage of necessity and pleasure is 22-mile-long Lake Berryessa, in northeastern Napa County, 70 miles north of San Francisco.

As late as 1957, the lake site was occupied by fields of waving grain, and by the little frontier town of Monticello. Then the U.S. Bureau of Reclamation, spurred by appeals from farmers to the east, dammed

Deer in velvet. Mendocino and Lake counties,
of all in the game-rich Redwood Empire,
yield the most bucks to hunters.
Occasionally complaints by landowners
about deer depredations in orchards
or young forests bring state permits for doe
(or "antler-less") hunts—and
also cries of outrage from sportsmen
who differ with this theory of herd control.

86

A string of black bass from Clear Lake. Best fishing is in the tule-and-willow fringed shallows along the lakeshore. Smallmouth black bass, popularly known as "bronzebacks," weigh up to six and eight pounds, and put up a notable fight for their size.

Launching an outboard motorboat at Lake Berryessa, manmade pond with a 165-mile shoreline in eastern Napa County. For several years after the lake was opened in 1959, it produced bass of surprising size: natural feed from the drowned fields fattened the fish at an unprecedented rate.

up lively Putah Creek. Within two years, they had created a body of water whose winding inlets gave it a shoreline of 165 miles, a width of 3 miles in spots, and depths up to 275 feet.

The bureau turned administration of the new lake over to Napa County, which runs it as a county park. The county then leased resort areas to seven private concerns. These operate facilities ranging from launching ramps and snack-bars to trailer parks and motels.

Lake Berryessa was a success almost before it was filled. Its proximity to the Northern California population centers brought thousands of eager boatmen, anglers, and campers in 1959. In 1963 the 22-mile-long lake hosted nearly 1½ million.

*Water skiing on Lake Berryessa. Nearly 2 million
recreationists are logged here each year.*

Over the west hangs the pungent haze from a million cookouts, the smacks of myriad golf balls, the steady click of thousands of credit cards being recorded.

Westerners take their relaxation seriously, and go to great lengths to find the good life they have out-lined in their dreams.

Close to 7,000 new cars are registered in California weekly. Most of California's 18 million proponents of the good life push out onto the highways during the summer, in a frantic quest for playing room.

They spend half a billion dollars for hunting and fishing trips. In 1963, they bought 1,611,639 fishing licenses, three-quarters of a million hunting permits (and lugged home 65,000 deer), and paid taxes on 300,000 boats.

Some of them realize their dreams of open hunting space in Lake and Mendocino Counties. Deer by the hundred are shot and tagged annually in the state's 50,000-acre Cow Mountain preserve west of Clear Lake.

There is even big game, of a sort. Last year hunters in the region slew 64 black bears.

*Carson Mansion, now the private
preserve of the Ingomar Club, Eureka. Completed 1886.*

Hot Stuff

Under the redwood-crowned earth of the Mayacmas mountain range, molten magma lies close to the surface.

Geysers and hot springs abound in the counties of Napa, Sonoma, and Lake, but nowhere with such force as in Devil's Canyon, 20 miles west of Geyserville in northern Sonoma County.

Not a true geyser, but a steam well, spudded in at Devil's Canyon in 1955. When the belcher let loose, it hurled stones 3,500 feet in the air, later subsided to a steady flow of 150 feet of steam. Pacific Gas & Electric Co. uses such wells for its geothermal power plant at the geysers.

The canyon was discovered first by Indians, who used to put ailing braves on platforms over steamy outlets until the parboiled patients recovered—or died. In 1847, trapper William B. Elliot, chasing a wounded bear, stumbled on the canyon's spouts and fumaroles. Not long thereafter two enterprising innkeepers, Levy and Ewing, erected a hotel nearby and aided by that devil's coachman, Clark Foss, attracted a brisk trade to the curative waters, and to such picturesquely named wonders as the Devil's Teakettle and the Witches' Cauldron.

Among the clientele over the years were three Presidents—Grant, Theodore Roosevelt, and Taft—as well as Lotta Crabtree, Nellie Melba, Mark Twain, Giuseppe Garibaldi, and the Prince of Wales—later Edward VII. In the 1870's the geysers led Yosemite in popularity.

In 1921, a Healdsburg firm tried to harness the canyon's steam and convert it to electricity. Eight wells were drilled by the Geyser Development Co., but underground pressure overpowered human technique, and the landscape was sprayed with casings. Subsequent attempts led to a better-conceived program by Pacific Gas & Electric Co. in 1959, and the canyon became the site of America's first geothermal power station.

Fashionable resort life at the Geyser Springs Hotel in the 1870's, by famed photographer Eadweard Muybridge. Muybridge in 1874 pistoled his wife's lover near another geyser resort, Calistoga, but was acquitted. About this time he also pioneered motion pictures by photographing a running horse for Governor Leland Stanford.

A comfortable start to the geysers and the wine valleys in the 1870's was made by steamer. This is the Antelope side-wheeler at Donohue's Landing, south of Sonoma about 1878. She plied the Sacramento River and carried the first Pony Express rider from Sacramento to San Francisco.

THE GIANT
th 56 ft. Diameter 8 ft.
SEQUOIA GIGANTEA
CALIFORNIA REDWOOD

*Six million years ago an eruption of Mount
St. Helena turned a grove of giant redwoods
to stone west of Calistoga. Today they are
a tourist attraction, largest petrified
trees on earth. A small fir grows from soil
imbedded in this fallen monarch.*

Old church, Bodega;
northwestern Sonoma County.

South Coast and Rivers:
Sonoma and Mendocino

Although no longer *terra incognita,* the topography of this coast inhibits easy familiarity. Cliffs rise streaming from the sea, the coastline is sculpted by "dog-hole" inlets—ports where a dog would be hard put to turn around, though lumber ships did. A two-lane road writhes along the edge of the Pacific.

"If we could flatten out these hills," cried one logger in the 1890's, "the forest would cover all of the United States and part of Texas." Nowadays realtors lament that if Anchor Bay was near Malibu they could sell it by the inch.

Nature conspired long ago to frustrate such ambitions. The untamed look that charms the visitor owes everything to weather and inaccessibility. Fog and chill seas repel the Dolce Vita types, and the surfers. Instead "artists come to escape and escapists come to hide." Neon finds blinking unprofitable.

Hemmed in for a century, the natives make a fine art of minding their own business. They are descendants of the Yankee loggers who built towns like 'Quoddy or Kennebunkport. But the exurbanites have established a beachhead, and realtors watch eagerly as newcomers mine the beaches for driftwood and cocktail chat. "Up the Coast for the weekend" has status.

Old-timers and the few outlanders who hoped to keep the Coast their secret are alarmed. Peering through the summer at cars crawling up the roads, they seem to see the vanguard of the Jet Age, looking for a new Waikiki.

Waves, Sonoma Coast State Park.

Russia's Farthest-flung Colony

The sight of the strange six-sided steeple and the crooked double cross of Eastern Orthodoxy makes it possible to believe California might have become Russian.

A redwood-slab chapel, two boxy blockhouses, a stockade, and the low manager's house overlook the gray Pacific at Fort Ross.

On this barren tableland, two hours by sports car from San Francisco, 700 subjects of the Czar once toiled to realize Russian dreams of Pacific domination. They might have pulled it off—except for the gopher and the sea otter.

In the first decade of the nineteenth century, Russia's eastward surge of empire was cresting in Alaska. Fur supported this astonishing colonial effort. Alaskan sea otter pelts were fetching $300 from luxury-loving Chinese mandarins. But fur and food were running short at Sitka, so the manager of the Russian-American Fur Company, Alexander Baranov, sent expeditions down the coast to California.

Spain had nominal ownership here, but peg-legged Ivan Kuskov, Baranov's chief emissary, knew Spain had no soldiers north of San Francisco. Kuskov found a rocky inlet above Bodega Bay, gave the local Indians some beads in trade for a thousand acres, and set to building a log fort. He called it Ross, the ancient term for Russia.

In one year, 200,000 otter pelts went back to Sitka. The Russians set Aleut hunters ranging out to the Farallones to spear and skin the aquatic mammals. They would capture an otter cub and hold it, screaming, until its parents surfaced to be harpooned.

Fort Ross chapel, through pines, looking seaward.

Crops were planted, including sloeberries to flavor vodka. Cannon (some seized from Napoleon) bristled from the blockhouses. In San Francisco, Navy Lieutenant D. I. Zavalishian intrigued to ally the mission fathers with Holy Russia against the godless Mexican expropriators. Czar Alexander I, doubling as president of the Russian-American Company, issued an imperial ukase forbidding the North Pacific to all except Russian ships.

Alarmed, President James Monroe countered with his Doctrine of 1823. Foreign despots were warned off the continent. Yet to Kuskov, Washington was far away and of little consequence. Similarly, the siesta-minded Spanish, now remote subjects of troubled Mexico, posed puny obstacles to Fort Ross ships and cannon. California was open to Russian conquest.

At this point animal economics took a hand, or perhaps a paw. Years of overkilling had almost exterminated the otter herds, and each year saw fewer skins for Sitka. Now gophers, "underground rats," began eating the Muscovite crops. Faced with bankruptcy and starvation, the Russian-American Company took a sterner look at its California colony. It was, the directors decided, a liability. The new Czar, Nicholas I, concurred. There was too much private enterprise in the company to suit his autocratic views.

In 1840 the last company manager, Alexander Rotchev, sold the fort to Captain Johann Sutter, Swiss overlord of Sacramento. The price was $30,000. Rotchev's wife, blonde Princess Helena, before she left, asked Sutter to save her little greenhouse where she had spent so many happy hours. The boyars then sailed away, and slow decay set in at Fort Ross.

After World War II, state parks workmen began rebuilding the old outpost. They picked up the hand-hewn timbers which, being of redwood, were almost intact. The Russians had used pegs and bolts instead of nails, and so did the restorers. The stockade had been put up without chalk line or plumb bob, and it was reerected that way. One of the original chapel bells, cast in St. Petersburg, turned up in the Petaluma firehouse, and it was rehung at Fort Ross.

Each Fourth of July, bearded metropolitans from the Russian churches of San Francisco celebrate Orthodox Mass in the little chapel. Their chants, their robes, their incense evoke Kuskov's day. A hundred thousand motorists visit the historic monument each year, shivering in the museum where once a Russian princess lived.

And the otter? After a century of eclipse, a small herd turned up off the Monterey Coast in 1937. Protected by the state, one day they may even return to the gray seas off Fort Ross.

95

The Russians left few legacies in California.
One is a famous place-name: the Russian River, which Kuskov's
canoemen called the Slavianka. Rising in the Coast Ranges
north of Ukiah, the Russian waters a sizable redwood forest
near the Coast. South of here Captain Stephen Smith
built California's first steam-powered sawmill in 1843.
In 1859, George Guerne and Tom Heald came to the Russian
River and began cutting the giants to feed the demand for
building materials in San Francisco. This busy scene
at Guerneville shows axmen attacking a redwood from scaffolds,
horse and bull teams hauling away redwood sections.
Photo was made by Joseph H. Downing, who came to Healdsburg in 1857.

When the San Francisco & North
Pacific Railway and the rival
North Pacific Coast Railroad
pushed up to the Russian River
in the 1870's, they brought
picnickers who transformed the
river from a logging camp to a
genteel summer resort. As the
supply of readily available timber
dwindled, pleasure replaced
planks in the local economy.
At right, a water carnival flourishes
at Monte Rio in the early 1900's.

96

Unique among amateur theatricals is the annual Grove Play staged by San Francisco's Bohemian Club in its private redwood forest near Monte Rio, on the Russian River. Notables such as the late President Hoover turned up carrying a spear in the club's costumed extravaganzas, like this one in 1925. Women are rigidly barred from the Bohemian's summer encampments, but female population in resorts outside predictably increases during the two-week stay.

The redwoods retain their wonder for the casual vacationer. At Guerneville in crinoline days, someone built this summerhouse into a giant whose trunk had been partly hollowed out in some forgotten fire. Near Guerneville ("guern"—never "gurney") is Armstrong Redwoods State Park, 440 acres, with amphitheater for concerts, and a picnic ground.

Big Sandy Beach at Monte Rio. Summer homes line the far shore while swimmers and sunbathers swell the summer population. The Russian River has treacherous potholes and swift currents despite its placid mien and demands respect.

Knife-and-Fork City

Take 500 pounds each of beef, pork, and veal; 60 fricassee hens, a few dozen onions, two crates of Swiss chard, plenty of rosemary, salt, pepper, olive oil, eggs, Peccorino cheese—and you have one week's raw materials for Occidental's principal industry.

Occidental produces ravioli in Herculean quantities. Also chicken cacciatore, scallopini, crab cioppino. Its epicurean ravioli filling, one ton of it a week, is described above. In addition, Occidental consumes hundred of dozens of frying chickens, tons of beef and veal, almost a thousand gallons of wine, mountains of salad, pasta and zucchini fritters every few days.

Since this dietician's nightmare is produced in a town of less than 800 souls, located in western Sonoma County, how does Occidental stay afloat in such a sea of food?

The answer lies in export. Occidental's three famous Italian restaurants serve 6,000 to 8,000 meals every weekend in the eating-out season. On Easter Sunday and Mother's Day parking space is non-existent in "Calorie Canyon," the two narrow streets that run the length of the little town. Cars from every part of Northern California jam the place; their owners will be inside the Union Hotel, Negri's or Fiori's, spreading themselves and helping spread the fame of Occidental, the knife-and-fork city.

"Calorie Canyon" has made food its business since the old logging days when it was successively known as Meekers, Summit, and Howards. When M. C. "Boss" Meeker's woodsmen were sawing redwood logs south of the Russian River a century ago, John Gobetti's Golden Gate Hotel was the best-patronized of the town's eight saloons. Gobetti's talent as a chef brought fame to the Golden Gate; he served Paul Bunyan-sized dinners for two bits (wine included), 35 cents on Saturday nights and Sundays. Soon Gobetti took over the Union Hotel, too.

Redwood logging waned in the 1890's. Occidental (so it was named, for no particular reason, by a church congregation) seemed unlikely to survive. But frugal Italian farmers found they could buy logged-off land cheap. They introduced the Old Country practice of charcoal-burning, to clear the property. Soon stacks of charcoal were piled high at the North Pacific Coast Railroad depot, awaiting shipment down the narrow-gauge line to San Francisco. The hardworking Neapolitans, Florentines, Piedmontese all liked to eat, and they introduced Italian recipes at the saloon-restaurants. In no time at all, Occidental became known as *the* place to dine. And so it has remained.

In the early days, the North Pacific Coast Railroad used to carry excursion trains up to the Russian River from its Sausalito and San Quentin terminals on the Bay. Occidental frequently was a dining or

Signs at Negri's Original Occidental. Negri's burned to the ground one night in August, 1966, and will be rebuilt.

Main Street, in fact the only street, in Occidental.

Dinner at the Union Hotel. A slow night, after 9 P.M.

picnic stop on the route to Monte Rio. Natives of San Francisco's Barbary Coast were among those who delighted in these woodsy weekends, and sometimes mayhem and intoxication ruled the rails. In his nostalgic *Redwood Railroads,* the late Gil Kneiss describes the scene: "Shills staged sham fights for pickpockets who frisked the crowds that gathered, while urchins hanging around the picnic grounds had no trouble learning what came after the birds and the bees." After many colorful years, the line was discontinued in 1935.

Occidental has frequently been hit hard by fires. The most recent gutted Fiori's, but the owners—Mrs. Anthony Fiori and Mr. and Mrs. George Fiori—started rebuilding immediately. Negri's—also known as The Original Occidental—has burned several times. Mr. and Mrs. Joe Negri and their sons Albert and Joe, Jr., have expanded each time they rebuilt. For some unaccountable reason the Union Hotel, built in 1879, has been spared. It carries its original gingerbread trim with pride; its hitching rings are still sunk in the sidewalk outside.

Occidental is a town of cousins, and if one café runs short of ravioli, the other two lend enough to cover the emergency. One of the biggest families is the Clan Gonnella. Daniel helps run the Union Hotel. A photo in the town grocery store shows a local baseball nine which includes five Gonnellas.

Since the town does nothing to advertise itself, strangers who view its Gargantuan culinary establishment in full swing often find it incredible. A Los Angeles editor came to Occidental reluctantly because he couldn't see how such a small place could provide him with a story. One seven-course dinner at Negri's made a believer out of the newsman, and he described Occidental's charms in an enthusiastic Sunday column.

Not the least of these charms is a genuine hospitality which has its roots in the Old Country. Owners, waitresses, bartenders—all greet customers with smiles and aplomb. "Party of thirty!" Mary Panizzera calls into her vast kitchen at the Union Hotel. Occidental is strictly "family style." Though there's a wine list in all three cafés, none provides a menu. Ordering is confined to a choice of chicken (cacciatore, usually), steak or duck; or sometimes to a brimming crab cioppino, Italian-sailor fashion. The genuineness of Occidental's welcome is attested by the size of the bill: around $1.20 for an enormous lunch, $3.00 or $3.50 for a seven-course dinner.

No wonder that when Occidental's customers undo their napkins they sigh and agree, *"Provate a mangiare una volta ad Occidental sicuramente rittarnerete."* Which freely translated means: "Once you eat at Occidental, you'll be back."

Ravioli machine and crew, Union Hotel. From left: Mrs. Raymond Panelli, Mr. and Mrs. Dan Gonnella, Mrs. Arthur East.

Now the Coast north of Fort Ross assumes a different aspect. This is the interior-exterior pool at new Timber Cove Lodge, with sculptured torso by Benjamino Bufano. Hewn-redwood hotel and restaurant reflect dramatic surroundings, are the forerunner of a new surge of tourism, weekend homes.

Pint-sized Benny Bufano collaborates with Dick Clements of Timber Cove Properties to drill foundations for Bufano's 85-foot statue, "The Expanding Universe," on the cliffs above the Pacific. Always controversial, Bufano is an ardent pacifist who chopped off his trigger finger and mailed it to President Wilson to protest World War I.

*Culture, too. A string quartet
performs on weekends during the summer
season at Timber Cove.*

Tons of native rock went into
construction of this $200,000 home built
north of Anchor Bay by Artist-Designer
Millard Sheets. Sheets's "Sea Lion"
at right overlooks rocks on which a
thousand live brethren bark and romp.

Pine and rocks near Timber Cove.

Harry Meiggs's Red Gold

Harry Meiggs was an alderman in Gold Rush San Francisco. He owned a pier which bore his name, near present-day Fisherman's Wharf.

In 1851, word came to Meiggs's Wharf of a silk ship from the Orient, aground on the Mendocino Coast. Her rich cargo would be a notable prize. Meiggs dispatched salvagers.

Harry Meiggs's men discovered not silk, but another kind of wealth on this wild and remote shore. Here were trees so tall they hid the sky, so broad 20 men couldn't span them with outstretched arms . . . a mother-lode of redwood for the taking, concluded Harry Meiggs. He had helped denude the East Bay Hills to get lumber for fast-growing, faster-burning San Francisco. Lumber was selling for $500 per 1,000 board feet and these new forests represented a fortune.

Beside the inlet at Big River, Meiggs set up a sawmill and shipped cargoes of redwood lumber back to San Francisco. A thousand "State of Maine-ers," homesick woodsmen disillusioned with the gold diggings, flocked to the great redwood groves to do the kind of work they were used to.

Back in San Francisco, Meiggs was struggling in a web of speculation. He forged city warrants to cover his debts, then fled to South America. There Honest Harry built the first railroad across the Andes, and made a new fortune. As his legacy to the Coast, he started a lumber boom that lasted more than half a century.

Big River, briefly Meiggstown, became Mendocino. Steamers from Seattle and San Francisco made it a regular port of call. Hotels sprouted along Main Street. Local Paul Bunyans nicknamed $20 gold pieces "Big River bits."

Harry Meiggs, founder of the coastal lumber trade.

*Log pond at The
Pacific Lumber Company mill,
Scotia, reputedly world's
largest redwood sawmill.*

*After a rain at
Bull Creek Flat
in Rockefeller Redwoods
State Park.*

Two miles south of Mendocino, New Englanders founded the town of Little River. Here Silas Coombs, a graduate of the lumber camps, established shipyards and sawmills, built and operated a dozen lumber schooners.

To the north, a town called Fort Bragg grew up about a frontier Army post. In surrounding woods the Union Lumber Company began operations, under Charles Russell Johnson, whose name is inextricably bound with the story of the great Sequoias.

Silas Coombs (far right) *with his logging team in the Albion woods, about 1869. "Dogger," with heavy maul, stands atop log ready to knock chain underneath and slow juggernaut's downward career. Bullwhackers carry sharp goad sticks to prod oxen. These were used instead of less-manageable bullwhips.*

Schooner Electra *on the ways at Little River, in Thomas Peterson's shipyard. Thirteen vessels were built here in the boom lumber days of the 1860's and 1870's. Silas Coombs built there, too; one schooner turned turtle and sank while being launched. The imperturbable Coombs scorned to interrupt his midday meal when they brought him the news. Nor, said his son, did Silas ever refer to his traitor chattel again.*

Glass Plates on the Frontier

Gold opened up the West, but redwood did the job for the Mendocino Coast.

Harry Meiggs's partners reeled when his fortunes foundered. They set their sawteeth to recoup. The California Redwood Manufacturing Company had commitments to provide 100,000 board feet each day for lumber-starved San Francisco. Jerome Ford and Edwards C. Williams soon had two mills screeching at Big River, the forerunners of a hundred redwood enterprises.

Mill fires, shipwrecks, and falling prices wiped out most of them. Fort Bragg, Greenwood, Whitesboro, Albion, Caspar, Cleone, Newport, Kibesillah, Westport, Rockport, Usal, Bear Harbor—all knew their Roman-candle paydays. The camera's eye shows us how they looked, for photography was pioneering then, too.

With tripods and black hoods, photographers like Carleton Emmons Watkins and Aurelius Ornando Carpenter scouted the woods and wharves, making a living by their image of industry and scenic beauty. By chance their precious prints and a few glass negatives survive.

Watkins' dedication and talent are only now appreciated. He came to San Francisco during the Gold Rush and apprenticed at a San Francisco portrait studio. Daguerreotypes (or tintypes) had been introduced in America about 1839, but by 1851 a better process had been developed—wet-plate photography. Using collodion solution, coating squares of fine glass, photographers made their plates on the spot. Then they exposed the wet plates in big box cameras, removed and developed them immediately after exposure. Watkins became a leader in this technique, winning first prize for landscape photos in the Paris Exposition of 1868.

Fort Bragg was a military post when Carleton Emmons Watkins photographed it in 1863. Ten sets of whitewashed military quarters rise beyond the picket fence and lounging soldiers. The post was established in 1857 to discourage marauding Pomos, but was abandoned a decade later when the remaining Indians were shipped off to Round Valley Reservation. The fort's founder, Lieutenant Horatio Gibson, named it for a comrade of the Mexican War, who went on to become a Confederate general. In 1884, C. R. Johnson lived in the old hospital, left.

106

Dense stand of Sequoia Sempervirens
*in Mendocino County, probably
Montgomery Woods, west of Ukiah,
captured on glass by A. O. Carpenter.*

When his bread-and-butter portrait work permitted, he forsook the cities and cruised the West on muleback, lugging his cumbersome camera and collapsible darkroom. Watkins' photographs of Yosemite are exquisite. Each leaf, each pebble seems etched in crystal. His images of the Central Pacific Railroad and the Comstock Lode are historic gems.

In 1863, someone suggested he portray the redwood coast, so he packed up and headed for Mendocino and Fort Bragg. In a few weeks, he made 53 prints of the woods, the ports, the Indians. Using a giant view camera with a 75-degree lens which he had made himself, Watkins produced contact prints measuring 18 inches by 22 inches. He was aiming at a published album, popular in those days.

A few of these prints are in museums, but a number of Watkins' glass plates melted in the San Francisco fire of 1906, some were scraped clean and used again, and others, sad to relate, became part of a greenhouse. The photographer died old and forgotten at Napa State Hospital in 1916. His impressions of the West on glass are his monument.

"C. R.," Giant in the Forest

The Comstock had Mackay and Fair, the Central Pacific had Stanford and Huntington. But Charles Russell Johnson was the titan of the redwood coast.

C.R., as he was called, came out from Michigan at 23 and in 1882, bought into a shaky lumber mill near Newport.

The system of operation was simple. Logs were cut in the spring and summer, hauled by ox teams to the rivers, floated down to the mills. Then schooners would freight the finished planks down to San Francisco.

But the hazards were enormous. There were fires in the woods, and in the mills. Rains made the steep, crude roadways impassable. The oxen were subject to mysterious illnesses; the loggers, to intemperance and riot. Floods hurled the logs past restraining booms and out to sea. Storms and reefs wrecked schooners by the score. Small wonder many companies went under.

C. R. Johnson saw it would take cash and staying power to win. Back in Michigan he persuaded his father and various wealthy lumbermen that 16-foot redwoods were no myth, and that logging them could be fantastically profitable. From the Michiganders, he raised the funds to start what became the Union Lumber Company. At Fort Bragg, only port big enough to handle large ships, C. R. built a wharf and a mill. He introduced band saws from the East to slice the heavy logs. He imported Chinese to dig tunnels and build a railroad 40 miles east to Willits.

All this was daring and costly. But C. R. persevered through depressions, through mill fires, through the disastrous earthquake of 1906. This epic tremor leveled his mill at Fort Bragg, but it also created a demand for redwood to rebuild San Francisco. This in turn financed the Union Lumber Company's comeback.

C. R. could see that Union's future was tied to its forests, and that the woods needed management to provide a constant harvest of trees. He instituted reforestation practices, or "tree farming," for which the lumber industry honors his name.

C. R. died in 1940. His company today is one of the world's three largest redwood operations, milling 116 million board feet in 1963, and reserving 208,000 acres in tree farms.

Charles Russell Johnson, founder of the Union Lumber Company. His grandson now heads the firm at Fort Bragg.

*Water towers and clapboard stores
survive at Mendocino, until lately remote and
forgotten on its Pacific cliffs.*

Bull teams moved raw lumber in the Mendocino redwoods. A. O. Carpenter's camera catches seven span of oxen pulling 12 big logs down a steep skid road near Fort Bragg. Brandishing his goad is the bull puncher at $100 a month the highest-paid man in the woods. Partway uphill is the sugler, whose job was to water down the path to make the logs slide easier, especially on level ground. Coming downhill, brakes had to be improvised. Sometimes the log train would gain express momentum and overrun the rear span, resulting in mashed cattle and blocked roads.

Jackscrews were used to roll big logs sideways, before the advent of steam winches and tractors. This is at Fort Bragg in the 1890's. C. R. Johnson recalled that "two men with a jackscrew could get a log out of a hole and turn it clear around."

110

*Laying the bed for a skid road.
Mammoth logs had to be dragged
lengthways over these bumpy paths by
ox-power, or by steam-donkey engines
(background). Photo made in Mendocino
woods by A. O. Carpenter about 1880.*

*Falling a 14-foot redwood in the 1880's, as
depicted by A. W. Ericson, Arcata photographer.
With crosscut saw (right) and double-bitted
felling ax, loggers sometimes took a week to drop
a giant like this. To avoid tree's swelling base,
they stood on tapered springboards driven
into the wood eight feet or more above the
ground. Forecut came first, then deep cut.
Nowadays few very large trees are
felled, and the job is done speedily on middle-sized
ones with power-driven chain saw and wedges.*

Albion Mill in the 1860's, by C. E. Watkins. Ferry in foreground provided sole means of traversing Albion River between Mendocino and Navarro. Now a long highway bridge spans the gulch from headland at left. Watkins' prints were used as models for the California landscape painter William Keith.

Winter log storage on Pudding Creek, north of Fort Bragg, in 1910. Dam (off photo, left) was built in 1906 to hold 20 million board feet of redwood.

It took 3½ days to fall this 17½-foot redwood near Northspur Camp on the Noyo River in January, 1933. Part of the choppers' job was to make falling bed out of smaller logs and branches so giant would escape damage during its crash to earth. This tree was selected to provide timbers for the old Yolo Causeway west of Sacramento. Aside from pilings, most of the wood for the three-mile causeway came from this single Mendocino Sequoia.

A redwood log makes a stirring splash as it hits the pond at Little River. Pond-tender, with pike pole, balances on boom.

Logging train in the woods near Albion, late 1880's. Steam was replacing bull-power, but rail construction cost up to $40,000 a mile. Trestles like this were raised with local timber. One over Jughandle Creek was reputed to be the world's highest, until it crumpled in the 1906 earthquake. Locomotive in this A. O. Carpenter print is the "Albion," 1885-model Baldwin 2-4-2T, property of the Albion River Railroad. The ARRR was bought and operated by Southern Pacific from 1907 to 1930. This road "lokey" served to the end.

Loading a schooner by wire chute at Signal Port (also known as Hardscratch), long-forgotten doghole 10 miles south of Point Arena. Lumber slid 200 feet or more down precarious greased chute, was arrested short of ship by the clapperman. Only when this functionary raised his trap did the cargo slip aboard. More than 20 of these chutes operated in the redwood coast's heyday, made necessary by the scarcity of good ports and rocky offshore. The "Scandinavian Navy" was skippered by fearless characters like Midnight Olsen, Portwine Ellefsen, Hoodlum Bob Walvig, and Rainwater Johnson.

Specially built steam schooners replaced their sail-powered
sisters in the 1890's. Still lumbermen labored to bring the ships
to the trees by the shortest route, and this Rube Goldberg
wharf at Westport, north of Fort Bragg, was a temporary
answer, 400 feet out over the rocks. Loading by cable are the
steam schooners Scotia and Prentiss.

Shortcut ashore: Captain Schuyler Colfax Mitchell, his
wife, daughters and a mate don Sunday best to ride sling from
the big schooner Irene to Noyo Wharf in 1915.
Irene was loading 900,000 feet of redwood for Australia. Airy
trip covered a quarter-mile, but the ladies preserved their
poise and their hats.

*Tandem horsepower pulls
lumber to waiting schooners
at Albion dock.*

Steam winch on the Albion Wharf loads redwood timbers for San Francisco.

116

*Lighthouse at Point Arena was one of
the tallest on the California Coast until
the earthquake of 1906 left it in ruins.
It was rebuilt a few years later, still
functions.*

Wire chute and bales of shingles at Point Arena.

Crashing surf on the redwood coast.

118

Most Cruel Sea

"Thrice ribbed in brass and oak his heart, who first dared trust a frail bark to the merciless sea." . . . Horace.

The booming ocean carved deep gashes in the redwood coast, left these tiny ports rimmed with rocks and cliffs so sheer no sane skipper would attempt them. Duncan's Cove, Russian Gulch, and Little River had the timber. But their tides and reefs "could be challenged only by the smallest of ships and entered by the most superb of pilots," says Author Jack McNairn, in his *Ships of the Redwood Coast.*

Many stout vessels came to grief on these shores starting with Cermeño's *San Augustin,* in 1595. Historian Wallace E. Martin of Eureka records 113 maritime disasters between 1850 and 1957 on the hundred miles of Mendocino coastline alone. A few Martin samples:

> The brig *North Bend.* Wrecked at Big River in November, 1855.
> The *Elizabeth Buckley.* Struck Wash Rock north of Point Arena in 1862.
> The S.S. *San Benito.* Lost off Point Arena in November, 1896; 24 drowned.
> The British steamer *Orteric.* Wrecked on Fish Rock in 1922.

There was a silver lining to some of these disaster clouds, at least for the coastal natives. When the S.S. *Dorothy Wintermote* smashed up at Anchor Bay in September, 1938, shore dwellers subsisted for a decade on her 1,400 tons of coffee, shortening, and soap.

Not all the coasting schooners ended with Davy Jones. Some rotted away in the estuary boneyards off Oakland when logging trucks replaced them after the last war.

Two have been preserved for posterity at San Francisco's Maritime Monument, at the foot of Hyde

Schooner Oakland *on the beach near Mendocino, June 24, 1924.*

Lumber schooner Bobolink *bound for San Francisco, fast in the rocks at Kent's Point, near Mendocino, March 24, 1898. The cook was lost overboard but* Bobolink's *deck cargo (185,000 board feet) was salvaged before she broke up.*

Above: *Steamer* Pomona, *foundered on the Fort Ross rocks in 1908. Standing by is the salvage schooner* Greenwood, *whose own saga ended years later on the Oakland mud flats.*

Saved from the wreck, Pomona's *nameplate adorns this cottage at Fort Ross.*

Street. They are the three-masted *C. A. Thayer* and the 951-ton steam schooner *Wapama*. For a few dimes, tourists may board these handsome relics in their last berth, reconstruct the doghole days.

The redwood coast shingle run was a preparatory school for Western shipping magnates.

Captain Robert Dollar was the prototype. He owned a sawmill at Usal, north of Rockport, and, to ship his products, he ordered the steam schooner *Newsboy* built at a San Francisco yard in 1888. Not much bigger than a launch, *Newsboy* was the first of Dollar's mighty fleet—60 freighters and passenger liners, the largest commercial armada to fly the American flag, and forerunner of American President Lines.

Oliver Olson and Charlie McCormick also built seagoing empires in the coastal trade. Their hammer-handed mates battled mutineers afloat and Finn loggers ashore with fine impartiality.

During Prohibition, some coastal crews supplemented their pay by smuggling liquor from Canadian or Mexican ports. Aboard the *Daisy Gadsby* one steward reputedly enjoyed an income several times that of the master's. Other steam schooners became widely famed in San Francisco, since when they made port they speedily converted to speakeasies for parched landlubbers.

Rum-running reached the proportions of a major industry along the redwood coast in this doleful era. Bodega Bay was a favored depot for night-landed case goods. The local coroner made frequent runs to Petaluma, 27 miles inland, tooling a hearse with curtains discreetly drawn.

Despite the high death rate at Bodega Bay, the town survived, and so did the customers at Petaluma and points south.

Steamship tycoon Robert Dollar founded his maritime empire with this tiny (208-ton) steam schooner, Newsboy, *shown here docked to pick up lumber at Fort Bragg in the 1890's. Dollar used her from 1888 onward to carry cargo from his mill at Usal, north of Westport, an inaccessible doghole.* Newsboy *sank after a collision with the larger* Wasp *on Humboldt Bay in April, 1906. She was the first steam schooner built with engines, her predecessors being sailing-ship conversions.*

Coast in Transition

By the Second World War, lumbering in the Mendocino forests was finished. Big River sawed its last logs in 1938. Mills at Albion, Greenwood, Ten Mile River were dismantled for scrap, or caught fire and became burned-out wastes.

Rust and rot caved in wire chutes that had loaded a billion board feet for San Francisco. Wharves collapsed, and wild roses choked the old saloons.

The proud down-Westers scorned to complain. They worked in the woods when there was logging, fished or took odd jobs when there wasn't. Always there was the sea. A famous Coast saying holds: "When the tide's out, table's set." Abalones and clams eked out many a family meal.

"Father Time and the Maiden" is Mendocino's most distinctive landmark, carved from
a redwood log by Eric Albertson in the late 1860's. It is the crowning ornament for
Mendocino's graceful Masonic Temple, where Albertson served four terms as master.
"Prince" Albertson was paid $1,000 for his five years' work in building the two-
story hall, which fee included the statues and elaborate wood carving inside.

The Coast knew hard times earlier and longer than the rest of California. Perversely, this paved the way for its present recognition. Under prosperity, ancient stores and houses might have been razed or remodeled. As it was, their Victorian charms were left untainted. Farms that would have yielded to road-side stands or tract homes kept intact their flocks of sheep, their split-rail fences.

When times were ripe, the artists, the nature-lovers, the world-weary discovered the Coast's beauty. Her long sleep had preserved her looks.

August A. Heeser, publisher of the Mendocino Beacon, *and dean of the state's weekly press, in his office before the vault which housed town's valuables when building was a bank. Heeser's father came to Mendocino in 1857, preceded him as publisher, also owned bank and general store. His son died in 1966 at 89.*

Hardy survivor: this Presbyterian Church at Mendocino, erected in 1858 from donations by Jerome Ford and William Kelly, two of the earliest lumber barons. In 1946, Hollywood used church in several scenes from Johnny Belinda, *and filmdom's rents paid for a new roof and foundation.*

Bill Zacha, artist,
teacher and entrepreneur,
with old water tower in Mendocino
which he remodeled as a three-story
atelier *for an artistic tenant.*

Mendocino has a joss house, too, one of two in Upper California. The other is a state historical monument at Weaverville.

It has a sea view! This 100-year-old residence, lacking modern plumbing but occupying a sloping half block in Mendocino, was offered for sale at $53,000. Property prices have skyrocketed in the last few years.

Hazy autumn in Mendocino. At right, the old Presbyterian Church.

126

Artists in Residence

For a generation that can pay more for nonobjective oils than Cadillacs, art is the new bellwether.

Serious art needs the proper atmosphere and pace. By 1960, in the eyes of the *avant-garde*, Sausalito, North Beach, and Big Sur had become too hectic, too commercialized. Many took flight.

Bill Zacha was among the first. Painter and teacher in Marin and San Francisco, he came to Mendocino for a weekend in 1957 and decided this was Parnassus West. Zacha got a job teaching in the local high school, made a $50 payment on a steep-gabled mansion, and moved his family in.

In May, 1959, Bill and six friends founded the nonprofit Mendocino Art Center in a bramble-covered mansion and held a work party to clean it up. Next year the center opened summer classes. Now it is in the black, and the original half-block is covered with classrooms abuzz with mosaic-gluers, weavers, sculptors, watercolorists, and mural daubers.

Mendocino's old-timers were leery of Zacha and his group. Loggers and fishermen goggled at the beards and black stockings, and failed to appreciate the free-form chatter, the midnight recorder solos. But in time the beatnik hangers-on drifted off, leaving a hard core whose object is to earn a living with integrity. When a certain amount of national attention focused on Mendocino, even the sourest native began to see that the artists meant life to the moribund village.

Now the Art Center has sprouted branches. Millhands at Fort Bragg, housewives at Gualala, book-keepers in Elk and Ukiah are finding outlet in painting and carving. Visitors flock in to buy pottery, mosaics, and prints for $5 up.

The town of Mendocino looks like it did to the lens of Carleton Emmons Watkins. Clapboard houses, false-front stores are living Currier & Ives. Three-story mansions shine with pastel paint. Pre-Zacha, they sold for $4,000. Now it's more like $40,000; and bring your own plumbing.

Artists-in-residence vary with the circumstances, but include (or have included) Dorr Bothwell, whose serigraphs hang in New York's Metropolitan and the Paris *Bibliothèque Nationale;* Kent Bowman, jewelery designer; Charles Stevenson, who does casein multiportraits; Hilda Pertha, painter and textile designer. Most of these teach at the Art Center.

Another group revolves around the Coast Gallery: Byron Randall and his wife Emmy Lou Packard, who own a gallery on Main Street opposite the ancient Presbyterian Church; Kenneth Brandon, former art director of a San Francisco advertising agency; David Clayton, another painter who helps support himself as a fisherman; sculptors Raymond Rice and Harry Crotty.

Bill Zacha muses about life in Mendocino on a reclining board in the Bay Wind Gallery. He told a national magazine he wants to help make the town "a place where people can get a simple but profound satisfaction out of living."

Cora Coombs Hervilla and a Coast watercolor at Little River Inn, built by her grandfather in the 1850's. More successful in her medium than most native artists, Mrs. Hervilla took up painting in 1960, now gets $100 or more for each picture from inn patrons.

Byron Randall and his wife Emmy Lou Packard display oils and prints outside their gallery on Main Street. Miss Packard worked with Diego Rivera on murals for the International Exposition in San Francisco (1939–1940). Randall is a former merchant seaman. The couple came to Mendocino in the vanguard of the art migration that transformed the old mill town.

A point of pride in Mendocino is the degree to which artists can support themselves through art. The Randalls say they are doing it: their gallery usually has a sprinkling of shoppers and buyers for his coastal paintings or her colorful wood blocks reflecting the influence of her mentor, Diego Rivera. Miss Bothwell's reputation brings custom to the Bay Wind Gallery, also on Main Street, with prices in the $50 range for serigraphs and perhaps $400 for oils. Zacha's watercolors supplement his dabblings in real estate and his remodeling of water towers for artists' ateliers.

Whatever the returns, the artistic life is fine and free in Mendocino.

As for the future, Dorr Bothwell muses: "The town is like an early Carmel. I intend to enjoy it until it is tourist-ruined. Then I shall find another place to live."

*Art gallery perches
atop laundromat at Mendocino,
while a painter
plies her brush on the balcony.*

*Statuary and ceramics
for a price. A Main Street
gallery in Mendocino.*

128

*Students of all ages
at the Mendocino Art Center.*

Above: *A steelhead breaks water, and odds are good he'll get away. South coastal rivers of the Redwood Empire—the Russian, the Gualala, the Garcia, the Navarro—are favorite runs for these oceangoing rainbow trout. Steelhead have a formidable reputation as freshwater fighting fish. When the runs commence in November, hundreds of diehard anglers head for the redwood country, happy if they get a strike. Landing a 10-pound steelhead is often an hour's hard work.*

Left: *This is what they caught in the 1890's: 90 pounds of steelhead taken in the Gualala River, a still life by A. O. Carpenter. So plentiful were fish in those days that centenarian Charlie Brown recalled his father pitchforking salmon out of the Navarro in the winter of 1860.*

130

*Like a fishing port in Maine or the Mediterranean, Noyo bristles
with masts. Commercial netting and canning are profitable most
of the time; in one recent year Noyo shipped eight million pounds
of salmon, sole, and rockfish. Seafood restaurants dot the
waterside. Federal millions will be spent on a breakwater for Noyo,
safest port for small vessels between Humboldt Bay and the
Golden Gate.*

131

*Fishing boats at rest
mirrored in Noyo Harbor.*

*Smug fisherman displays 30-pound king salmon
taken off Noyo. Port is center for party-boat
expeditions when salmon run in
late summer and fall.*

How to Deodorize a Skunk

Railroad fans from faraway states and foreign countries head for Fort Bragg when they get to San Francisco. They want to ride the Skunk.

This is the nickname given in 1925 to the California Western Railroad's gasoline-powered passenger railcar. Steam trainmen said its fumes were no better than a polecat's.

Now hauled by inoffensive diesel engines, supplemented in 1965 with a steam train, the Skunk carries more than 100,000 sightseers a year. From a business point of view, it has become that present-day rarity—a passenger operation that is profitable. The two-hour fun ride is world famous.

Over its 40-mile winding course, the Skunk passes through redwood forests, over 44 bridges and trestles (there used to be 115), and through two tunnels. In one steep spot, its switchbacks and bowknots cover 8½ miles to go a mere mile and a half.

California Western Railroad's Skunk car M–80 on Northspur trestle over Noyo River. There are three separate varieties of tramcars, latest one being acquired in 1963 from a Utah short line. In 1965 a steam locomotive was added.

Passengers take a water break at Northspur when the new steam "Super Skunk" pauses to replenish its tanks for the uphill climb toward Willits.

California Western was built by Union Lumber Company as a means of getting its products to Willits, where CWRR could connect with the present Northwestern Pacific. From 1885 to 1911, C. R. Johnson's men labored mightily to conquer the ridges, the rivers, and the forests. Finally they made it. As a courtesy to residents along the way, the first passenger car was added in 1925.

Following nationwide publicity in the 1950's, the polecat's tail now wags the lumber line. Once CWRR capitulated to the railroad buffs, it went all the way. In 1965 the company bought an old logging locomotive and four vintage passenger cars, refurbished them in scarlet and gold inside and out, and inaugurated a summer "candy run."

The steam "Super Skunk," as the new train is called, immediately proved more popular than its diesel predecessor, as thousands of tourists demonstrated a desire to ride behind a genuine Iron Horse.

Engineer surveys winding roadbed beside the Noyo.

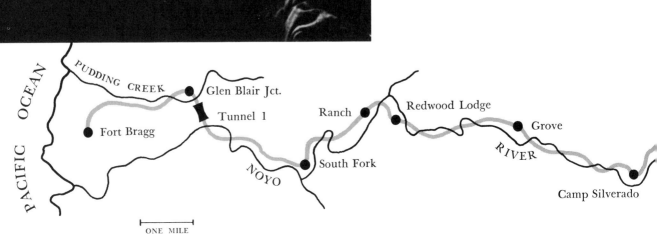

ONE MILE

Serendipity: the Coastal Inns

The look-of-Maine inns don't hand out keys, and the innkeeper, rubbing his hands beside the fire, doesn't rush forward to greet you. Outside the wind picks at the redwood shingles.

Yet you feel a welcome in this country. Most of the accommodations have been there long enough to get that lived-in look. The innkeeper is as blunt as an old caulk boot.

Ask Ole Hervilla about the roses that climb outside ancient Little River Inn. "Search me," Ole tells you. "We don't grow 'em, we fight 'em."

Down at the Gualala Hotel, where only steelhead fishermen used to stop, you're liable to get a paint-brush thrust into your hand. A few years ago, two dozen young suburbanites jointly bought the hostelry for $26,000, then started redecorating the early-lumberjack interior a room at a time, to each couple's specifications. The job is still in progress.

Queen of this part of the Coast is Heritage House. Loren Dennen's grandfather built the old place for the lumber-rich Pullen family when the cove underfoot was called Pullen's Landing. That was in 1877. When timber prices collapsed, the house decayed. Over the years it was used as a base for Chinese smugglers, for rumrunners, and for Baby Face Nelson when he was hiding from the Feds in the 1930's. Nelson was safe as long as he stayed at Pullen's Landing. He got caught when he tired of the lovely scenery and went elsewhere to look for action.

Scenery and sentiment tugged at Dennen and his wife when they returned to the Coast after living in Los Angeles. They bought the property on impulse, and began to scour the countryside for four-posters and potbelly stoves. Heritage House was an immediate hit when it opened, and has stayed that way. The Dennens are booked three years ahead on holidays. Part of their success is their stern refusal to regiment guests. "No one is going to hound you to play games," is the Dennen creed. Go beachcombing or walk in the woods. Or sit on the porch.

A local tourist attraction at Mendocino is the pygmy forest, full-grown cypress and pine only a foot tall. Acids in the soil have stunted a belt of forest only a mile from giant redwoods.

"Like a snake with the bellyache," Skunk route twists over river and mountain.

Several new resorts of this kind have opened, notably Timber Cove on the Sonoma Coast, a few cottage-type inns near Little River and Harbor House at Elk. There are some good motels in Fort Bragg.

The Dennens have taken over the Mendocino Hotel in the town of that name, redecorated it and leased it to young friends. Farther up the Coast, at bleak Westport, the Cobweb Palace is the place to stay—if you can find it open.

Innkeepers still are leery of the short season, but slowly the Coast is awakening, providing accommodations for the tourist tide.

View from Heritage House, most celebrated hostelry on the Mendocino Coast. Proprietor L. D. Dennen plants grass on the cottage roofs for insulation (and to atttract deer); furnishes "Scott's Opera House," "Country Store," and other chambers right out of Currier & Ives. He also keeps a succession of Ferraris.

THE MENDOCINO HOTEL

Est. 1873   MENDOCINO HOTEL   MENDOCINO CITY, CALIFORNIA

welcomes
the
visitor
to
Mendocino City
&
Adjacent Coast

Poster advertising Mendocino Hotel (above) is modern spoof with antique-type woodcuts. Town once boasted a streetful of hotels. Now—as Proprietor Bill Buckaloo points out—this is the survivor.

Above: *Beach north of Westport, which in turn is north of Fort Bragg. Here the Shoreline Highway turns inland to avoid the cliffs and gorges that reach north to Cape Mendocino.*

Left: *The harbor at Rockport, north of Westport, is so shallow and perilous that the Rockport Redwood Company built this 250-foot iron bridge out to an island so its ships could load. The span lasted only two years.*

Westport. Stores and post office.

Dip netter goes after surf smelt, which spawn on the coarse sand beaches of the Redwood Empire. Tasty catches are taken in the summer months, and a favorite fishing spot is at Juan Creek, near Westport.

Young forest near Branscomb.

*When lumber prices fell,
these company homes at Rockport
were vacated.*

*. . . and this new school
was boarded up before it opened.*

The Interior: Gun Law
in Round Valley

The Adult Western, complete with quick-drawing badmen, Injuns, and hardy sheriffs, seems as close as yesterday in parts of Mendocino County.

Comptche, Boonville, Covelo, Branscomb, and Laytonville were showdown country—and in some ways, they still are. Isolated, self-sufficient, the little interior towns tolerate strangers if they mind their own business. While San Francisco was gilding its ballrooms and strolling the Cocktail Route, men were facing men, Colts in hand, in these brushy hills.

The Old West is closest in Round Valley, 30 miles up a winding road northeast of Willits. The great white oaks and lush green pastures of Round Valley's big ranches, suggest the manorial estates of Surrey or Shropshire, but Covelo, all dusty streets and false fronts, proposes Dodge City or Deadwood.

Round Valley's history is dark and gory enough for any TV picture tube. When Sam Kelsey first saw it in 1854, seeking a trade route between Petaluma and Weaverville, he counted the campfires on the valley rim and estimated 20,000 Yuka Indians lived there. "Hookum Holt," Land of Big Water, they called it.

In time the last hunted Yuka would tell an Army agent: "We have lost faith in everything but death." Yankee squatters and vagabond hunters amused themselves by pot-shooting the Yukas, raping their squaws, kidnapping their children for sale into bondage. When the Indians resisted, massacres were organized.

In one New Year's Day frolic, a posse slew 50 unarmed Yukas—men, women, and children. One considerate settler even moved his wife to a relative's home beforehand so she wouldn't hear the gunfire.

Soldiers were summoned to keep the peace, but Army Lieutenant Edward Dillon drew sharp criticism from the poachers because he conceived it was also his duty to protect the Indians from the ravagers. The government in 1859 had compounded the trouble by resettling in Round Valley 1,000 Indians from widely scattered tribes. The uprooted natives fought among themselves awhile, then their various tribal cultures merged and disappeared.

By 1873 the Indians had ceased to be a problem—the troublesome ones were dead. Still there was no lack of entertainment in Round Valley. In *Harper's* Magazine that year a traveler reported: "Covelo . . . is the gathering place for a rude population which rides in on mustang ponies whenever it gets out of whiskey. The bar-rooms at Covelo sell more strong drink in a day than I have seen elsewhere. Shooting formerly was common, but it has gone out of fashion because most of the men are excellent shots, and the amusement was dangerous."

Pomos at Round Valley, wearing woodpecker-quill headdresses. A few of this tribe of basket-weavers also survive at Clear Lake.

John Hitt, one of Round Valley's surviving Indians, at his home place about 1939. Part of the valley and its hills to the north are still reservation, one of two remaining in Northern California. The tribal council occasionally meets in an old schoolhouse.

To the east of Round Valley lies the Middle Eel-Yolla Bolly Wilderness, unspoiled range for hunters, fishermen, and trail riders. Here are Bear Wallow Camp and Tantrum Glade, and 7,000-foot Anthony Peak, which is destined for winter-sports development. A graveled Forest Service road over 5,000-foot Mendocino Pass connects the region with the San Joaquin Valley near Willows.

In such a society, one ruthless overlord rose to dominance in the 1880's. This was George E. White, bearded giant who built a homestead into a 150,000-acre cattle empire. White was reputed to be the richest rancher in California, and his mansion near Covelo the finest north of San Francisco, with crystal chandeliers, music and billiard rooms. White held control of his acres by hiring a gang of desperadoes; of him a deputy attorney general said: "It was only necessary for him to intimate that [an enemy] be removed, and it would be done."

White had his enemies, including Ves (for Sylvester) Palmer, a rival rancher. One of Palmer's henchmen was Jack Littlefield, a cowboy of independent temper. Littlefield crossed White while the latter was embroiled in bitter divorce proceedings with his third wife. One September day in 1897, while Littlefield was on the trail north of Round Valley, he was arrested by Constable Baylis Van Horn and a deputy, charged with the murder of a neighbor. Handcuffed, Littlefield was escorted toward Covelo. On the trail, masked gunmen ambushed the trio, took Littlefield from the law, shot him and hanged him to a tree.

A coroner's jury all but closed the case, though it suggested the lawmen might somehow be implicated. But the masqueraders had been imprudent—they had seized Littlefield in the jurisdiction of Trinity County Sheriff Tom Bergen. Fearless and aggressive, Bergen in his turn bushwhacked Van Horn and two other suspects, toted them back to Weaverville for trial.

After a lengthy court session which literally bankrupted little Trinity County, Van Horn, his deputy, and five other men were convicted and imprisoned. White was never tried, but his name came up again and again, and the San Francisco newspapers had a field day with his "principality" and his "palace," his hired guns and his documented defiance of the law and of humanity.

Indeed, Round Valley won such a name that the story was told of an Oakland judge who informed a miscreant: "Prison is not severe enough—I'll send you to work in Round Valley." To which the prisoner replied: "Not that—hang me, Judge!"

White survived the trial, but he died in 1907, swindled of most of his empire by a spiritualist and the fourth wife she found for him. In his colorful *Tales from the Redwood Empire*, Dr. Hector Lee tells of White's connection with the Littlefield murder. Descendants of the principals still live in Round Valley, according to Dr. Lee, and to this day the story is a touchy topic.

Six-guns and war chants are stilled in Round Valley. Beef cattle graze in the belly-high forage, and the remaining redskins drive pickup trucks and wear store-bought Levis. Round Valley's violent past is paling, but the image still clings.

In 1959, a Santa Rosa developer announced plans for a "70,000-acre" (or was it 70,000-home?) super-community in the green valley. He wanted to capitalize on history, and suggested renaming Covelo "Frontier."

The town that remembers real range wars and Indian massacres was not impressed.

They Dig Boont Ling

The shoveltooth was at a sharking match when the telef rang, calling all kimneys to help dreek a jeffer.

This, in the esoteric and unique dialect called Boont Ling, is translated, "The doctor was playing cards when the phone rang, calling all men to help put out a fire."

Boont Ling is spoken nowhere else on earth except in the seaward-slanting Anderson Valley of southern Mendocino County. It is a manufactured jargon, like pig Latin, invented by Boonville youngsters in the early 1900's to befuddle their elders. Boont Ling survives today in Boonville, where half the population (800) digs the Boont for kicks.

If you hear someone talking about "ottoing," this means work; "dulcey" is candy; a "moshe" is a car; an "airtight," a sawmill; "frati" is liquor; and an "applehead," a girl. "Charling a broady" means milking a cow; one who "pikes to Boont for a hedge" is traveling to Boonville for a haircut.

Much of the lingo is based on nicknames for local characters. A shoveltooth is a physician because an early doctor had prominent bicuspids. A bear-man is a yarn-spinner because a noted storyteller also hunted bears. Like pig Latin, proficiency comes with practice in Boont Ling. Try this simple exercise:

"In '26, Pine Limb harped to the highpockets, 'We have ball gannows in Boont. Let's dehig ourselves

Fern Canyon, delicate jewel north of Orick,
its sheer banks tightly covered with native sword fern,
is now a part of Prairie Creek Redwoods State Park.
In 1965 the former owner, The Pacific Lumber Company,
gave it to the people of California.

and have a beamsh so everyone can deek.'" In other words: "In 1926 Tom Ruddock said to the town moneymen, 'We have fine apples in Boonville. Why don't we spend some money and have a show so everyone can see how fine?'"

And they did. And this is how the Anderson Valley Apple Show—the *Gannow Beamsh,* that is—got its start.

Rodeo at Covelo. Nearby is the Frontier Bank, once operated by a colorful lady financier whose casual habit was to leave large sums of cash in her car when in San Francisco on business. When it was towed off for overparking, the banker calmly reclaimed the vehicle and the money with the comment she considered folks everywhere as honest as they are in Covelo.

Grace Hudson, the Pomos' Remington

The Pomo Indians don't fit the television mold, but they were genuine, significant primitives. They are not part of the Great American Indian myth, like the fierce Sioux, the Apaches, or the Comanches of the Plains. But around the turn of the century a Ukiah doctor's gentle wife painted the Pomos and their children, and through her work these humble people survive.

Grace Carpenter Hudson, daughter of the photographer Aurelius Ornando Carpenter, painted more than 600 Indian portraits. Her subject was the Pomos—"diggers," as the frontiersmen scornfully dubbed them. "Where others saw filth and grime, she recognized simplicity and beauty," said her biographer. Mrs. Hudson particularly noted the Pomo affection for children and specialized in this aspect of tribal life. In a television script based on her art, David Grieve reports some of her findings: "A woman who has a baby spends practically all her time playing with it. . . . Her mother or some older person really cares for the baby, leaving her the simple enjoyment of him." Pomo infants' toys were carefully made, suggesting old legends or future activities like hunting.

Grace Hudson's method of obtaining models was unique: she would hire the papoose's mother to clean house for her. While the mother was busy, Mrs. Hudson would offer to take care of the solemn-eyed baby, then paint his portrait. This was in the Hudsons' artistic beamed home, "Sun House," which still stands in Ukiah.

Recognition came to Grace Hudson when her painting of a Pomo child, "Little Mendocino," was exhibited in 1893 at San Francisco and at the Chicago World's Fair. Critics thought her canvasses over-sentimental, but the lay public disagreed. She died in 1937, and today her work is widely scattered, but greatly loved. "Little Mendocino," fittingly enough, is in the collection of the California Historical Society.

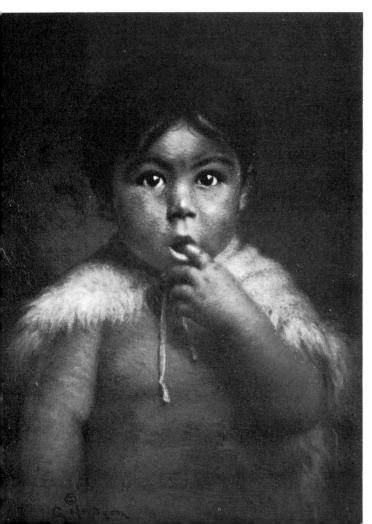

"Ka-wi-lote, *the unnamed baby," by Grace Carpenter Hudson. Pomos laced infants in tule (reed) mats until they received their name, after which a child was considered a separate being and was entitled to a transport basket. This baby's mother had a basket ready but wanted to delay naming until the painter (called by the Pomos Mad-tha-ku) returned from a trip to Chicago, and could do its portrait. Hence the child remained unbasketed and unnamed. As weeks went by, other Pomo families jeered that the baby was too big to be a no-name Ka-wi-lote, and its own mother was embarrassed. Finally when Mrs. Hudson returned, she gave the mother a fine white baby buggy from her own attic, and from that day Ka-wi-lote took on an additional meaning—opulence. This child therefore always was known as Ka-wi-lote. Painted in 1917.*

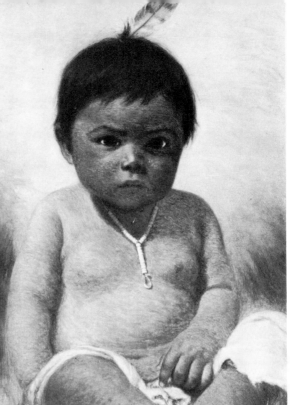

Indian child with an oak-ball toy, by Grace Hudson. Painted 1919.

Small Pomo brave with owl feather and bead necklace. By Grace Hudson, 1926.

Cha Bok and Kay-Kay-Pum *take their pipe-smoking and basket-weaving seriously for the artist. Pomos were famous basket-makers, used them as cooking and storage utensils. The weaving was as fine as Panama hats, and incorporated traditional patterns such as the quail's topknot.*

"The Boss" tousles his Pomo mother's hair. By Grace Hudson. Child portraits by this artist currently bring $3,000 or more. A few years ago they were largely ignored.

Badmen and Good

Just as colorful is the history of the regions around Ukiah and Willits.

In Willits, a gunfight took place in which six men died in 15 seconds. As late as 1907, an Indian shot up the town after warning two constables to take cover, which they prudently did.

Then there was Doc Standley, undersheriff and bulldog enforcer. In 1879 four outlaws, aiming for a lumber payroll, slew two deputies east of Fort Bragg. Doc Standley took out after the suspects. Riding across mountain and river, he barely slept until he had rounded up the gang, miles away in Butte County. Doc's son became a four-star admiral, chief of naval operations and ambassador to Russia in World War II. The Standley name survives in a state redwood park northwest of Willits and on a street in Ukiah.

Ukiah means "Long Valley" in the Indian tongue. In this long valley years ago settled Carl Purdy, whose reputation as a naturalist is second only to Luther Burbank's. Here too is the International Latitude Observatory, one of five in the world. (The others are in Maryland, Japan, Turkestan, and Sardinia.) Northeast of Ukiah is Lake Mendocino, which was created in 1957 by damming the Russian River. It is five miles long, a popular spot for boating, fishing, and water sports.

On the sweeping grade between Ukiah and Willits is Ridgewood Ranch, now property of a church but once the bluegrass spread of millionaire motorman Charles S. Howard. Such famous racehorses as Seabiscuit and Kayak II romped here. Howard's son Frank was killed in an accident on the ranch, and in his memory his father built the hospital at Willits.

Holidays were fun in Ukiah in the 1880's. This is a parade on State Street, from a photo by Aurelius Ornando Carpenter. A Vermonter, Carpenter settled in Potter Valley in 1859, helped found The Mendocino Herald, *the country's first newspaper. He published several papers including the Ukiah* City Press, *learned photography and took notable pictures of the redwoods and coastal shipping. He served in various government posts and died at 83 in 1919.*

Big Foot, Tall Tales?

Some men call it Big Foot, or *yeti,* or the Abominable Snowman. The Indians of 1840 in Mendocino County called it Ka-mets, said it was eight feet tall and fond of human flesh.

People who claim to have seen this hairy monster, half-man, half-bear, will brook no doubts. They know it exists. They point to 18-inch footprints, handprints a foot long, corroborating evidence from timber cruisers, housewives, and hunters. All testify to the Ka-mets' gigantic size, flat face, dangling arms, gentle habits. It has never harmed anyone, though it has frightened several almost to death.

For over a century, Ka-mets have been sighted or their tracks found in Humboldt, Trinity, Siskiyou, and Mendocino counties. Old settlers think there may be a colony of them, shy and bad-smelling, hiding in some remote wilderness canyon.

The most recent report came in 1962. Near Fort Bragg, outside the home of Mr. and Mrs. C. A. (Bud) Jenkins on the Willits Road, Mrs. Jenkins' brother-in-law, Bob Hatfield, spotted a shadowy figure staring over a low fence in the foggy darkness. At first he thought it was a bear. Then it stepped over the fence and loomed up next to him. Hatfield screamed, ran inside. The creature tried to push open the door, then shuffled off and disappeared.

Both the Jenkinses and Hatfield said they saw it plainly, described it just as frightened witnesses had done before. They measured its footprint, and a handprint. They smelled its pungent odor. It was no bear, and no man either, said the Jenkinses. It seemed as leery of humans as they were of its towering shape.

Some say the Ka-mets is a dream, a deliberate hoax for publicity, a bear, or someone's idea of a practical joke.

Those who have seen it, like Hatfield and the Jenkinses, know better. "It changed my wife and it changed my life," Jenkins told interviewers. The family was laughed at, and after a year of this, Mr. and Mrs. Jenkins moved away.

One serious student of the phenomenon has this to say: "From all the evidence of more than a century, there is something here profoundly alive, extremely active, and very elusive."

Indian legend makes Squaw Rock, beside the Russian River in southern Mendocino County, a point of interest for motorists on U.S. Highway 101. According to the story, an Indian maid spied her lover with another girl at the base of the sheer cliff, clasped a boulder and leaped down on them, killing all three.

Shoot-out at Little Lake

Election Day in Little Lake (now Willits), was October 16, 1867, and William Wesley Coates was doing what he liked best—fistfighting.

Backed by an armed contingent of the mean, tough Coates clan, Wes was pummeling an older man named Duncan, an in-law of the equally hard and dangerous Frost family. The Coateses and the Frosts were blood enemies.

Wes Coates knocked Duncan sprawling in the dusty street beside Simon Baechtel's feedstore. He bent down, took Duncan's pistol, and looked up into the steel-hard eyes of three Frosts. They had ridden into town unnoticed. Now they leaped from their horses, ready for trouble.

To Elisha Frost, 40, and his two nephews, Martin, 21, and Isom, 16, it appeared Wes Coates had gunned down their relative. The impression was reinforced by six more Coateses glowering behind the fighters in a half-circle.

In Little Lake Cemetery, east of Willits, monument marks the grave of Elisha Frost, lone member of his family killed in the fight against the Coates clan on October 16, 1867. In background: headstones of some of the five Coateses gunned down by Frosts.

150

The tension snapped when Abner Coates raised his shotgun and fired. Elisha Frost caught both barrels and dropped. As he did, he fired at Abner, missed, and killed Abner's son Albert, 21. Meantime Martin Frost opened up with his Navy Colt. Down went Wesley, Abraham, and Henry Coates, dead or fatally wounded. Sixteen-year-old Isom Frost also made his shots count, killing the Coates patriarch, Thomas, 60.

"My God!" cried Abner as his son fell. These were the only words spoken, witnesses remembered.

When the smoke cleared, the score was six dead and three wounded—Abner and James Coates, and Duncan. The entire action had taken only 15 seconds. By contrast, in the more famous gunfight at the O.K. Corral in Tombstone, Arizona, the Earp brothers and Doc Holliday took longer to kill only three men.

The Coates-Frost feud had been simmering for a long time. Some think it had its roots in the Civil War. The Coateses came from Wisconsin and the Frosts from Missouri. Others say it stemmed from Wes Coates's eye for one of Duncan's pretty daughters.

Whatever the causes, the gunplay didn't end the Frost propensity for trouble. Martin's brother Elijah, 29, was lynched as an outlaw at Ten Mile Bridge in 1879.

Martin himself was shot through the head by his own nephew, James, in 1884, in a dispute over land. "Did your uncle draw first?" someone asked. "I wouldn't be here if he had," replied James Frost, with proper respect for a marksman.

Isom Frost, who idolized his older brother Martin, trailed his nephew James and killed him from ambush the following year. For this Isom went to prison.

Isom Frost, the last of the feuders, eventually was released and lived on into old age, still remembered by a few elderly Mendocinans. They say he seemed gentle and kindly, his violent past remote and unreal. He always carried a rifle, but so did many on that frontier.

Before he died in bed Isom told a neighbor about the bloody Election Day:

"I didn't know what was happening, it happened so fast. When I saw Abner Coates draw up his shotgun and fire, and I heard Martin shooting, too, I just drew and fired.

"It seemed a matter of life and death, and I didn't know what was going on. I didn't want to kill nobody."

Joseph Coates's memory might dwell in the bosom of his friends, but few of his family survived to treasure it after the Frost-Coates street duel in Willits. Joseph lies with four Frost-killed relatives in the Little Lake boot hill.

Black Bart, Tidy Bandit

Charles E. Bolton stepped into the lobby of the Webb House in San Francisco one brisk morning in the late summer of 1877 and announced to the clerk that he would be away on a business trip for a couple of days.

"A proper gentleman," the clerk confided to loungers, "he neither drinks nor smokes. He's fussy if his room isn't spick-and-span, or if his linen is not laundered just right."

On August 3, 1877, a few days after Mr. Bolton stepped jauntily from his hotel, a Wells, Fargo and Co. stagecoach was halted between Fort Ross and the Russian River, some 60 miles north of San Francisco.

The stage driver, confronted by a shotgun-wielding bandit with a flour sack for a mask, yielded the company's strongbox. The driver later told authorities that the masked gunman gave his orders in a resonant tone. "Like someone," he described it, "talking into a rain barrel."

After helping himself to $300 in currency from the strongbox, the robber, to the amazement of the stage driver, began writing on a waybill which the driver subsequently handed to the sheriff. The officer was equally astonished when he read:

> "I've labored long and hard for bread—
> For honor and for riches—
> But on my corns too long you've trod,
> You fine-haired sons of bitches."

The quatrain of defiance was signed "Black Bart, the Po—8."

The doggerel was left at the scene of his first stage robbery by the quiet clerk whose real name was Charles E. Boles. Apparently he nursed a king-sized grudge against Wells, Fargo and Co.

Almost a year passed before Black Bart struck again, and once more the express company was the victim. On July 25, 1878, he robbed a stage operating between Quincy and Oroville. His haul was $379 in coin, a diamond ring, and a silver watch.

Black Bart's working getup on his second job was the same as he had worn on the first. His mask was a sack in which eyeholes had been cut, and his weapon was a shotgun. Once more he left behind a contribution of doggerel, somewhat expanded this time, but including the original quatrain.

In October, 1878, Black Bart staged his second stagecoach robbery in Redwood Empire country—the first being the Russian River caper. In the October job, the neat Mr. Bolton, or Boles, knocked over a stagecoach running between Covelo and Ukiah. Wells, Fargo declined to make public how much loot Black Bart obtained this time. However, since the bandit did not hold up another stage until 1880, it was believed the proceeds were considerable.

Charles E. Bolton, alias Black Bart.

In October, 1878, a masked bandit popped out from behind this rock on the road between Willits and Ukiah to relieve Wells, Fargo & Company's stagecoach of the money box. Today the boulder is known as Black Bart Rock.

(Black Bart Rock, scene of the October, 1878, holdup, is on the Redwood Highway, about 10 miles south of Willits in Mendocino County.)

By November, 1883, Black Bart had held up 23 more stages, and Wells, Fargo and Co. was thoroughly fed up. An $18,000 reward was offered for his capture.

Late in the autumn of 1883 a stagecoach, with a driver named O'Connell handling the reins, was rocking along the Sierra foothills between Milton and Sonora when it was suddenly forced to halt. The arresting figure again was Black Bart. Nudging O'Connell into the brush with a shotgun, the bandit then pried open the Wells, Fargo strongbox containing $4,800.

It was here, after six years, that Black Bart's luck ran out. While he was bundling the money away, a lad carrying a rifle sauntered up the road where he could be seen by O'Connell, but not by the highwayman.

O'Connell grabbed the boy's rifle and sniped at the surprised bandit, who fled into the underbrush. But as he scooted to safety, he dropped a silk handkerchief bearing the mark of a San Francisco laundry. This laundry mark led to his apprehension at his hotel by Wells, Fargo detectives.

Amiable and cooperative, Boles, who never molested a stagecoach passenger or fired a shot while engaged in his many robberies, pleaded guilty and was sentenced to serve seven years in San Quentin prison. He received time allowance for good behavior and was released from prison on January 23, 1888. After a brief visit to San Francisco, Boles departed and was last heard of in Visalia, south of Fresno.

In the summer of 1888, three more Wells, Fargo stagecoaches were held up. Express company officials believed these robberies were staged by the erstwhile Black Bart. However, he was never apprehended nor was he seen again in California.

Did Boles return to his wife, who lived in Illinois? While Boles was in prison, she wrote often to California authorities asking that he be released. Despite his long absence from his hearth, Black Bart was still cherished by his spouse.

She said he was a good man, and a tidy one.

153

Rails down the Eel

As late as the first decade of this century, goods and people moved into the northern Redwood Empire almost entirely by sea. The first settlements in Mendocino, Humboldt, and Del Norte counties sprang up around the few usable harbors. From there, logging railroads and a few crude wagon trails inched inland. Roads toward San Francisco Bay simply didn't exist. Few thought roads could ever be built over such bristling terrain.

The Indian wars of the 1850's and 1860's further delayed consideration of a north-south route. When these ended, cattlemen and lumbermen actually opposed such a road, the ranchers because it might bring in settlers to overrun their ranges, and the timber operators because, since they used the sea, they felt no need of a road and feared they would be taxed for it.

The Humboldt *Times* editorialized for a road. But when a vote to finance it in neighboring Mendocino County was forced in 1863, it lost 1,038 to 34.

Still, sea commerce was never ideal. Storms and adverse tides interrupted waterborne communications for weeks at a time. As towns like Eureka developed, the demand for a land route grew stronger. Almost simultaneously, the first probes for railroads and stage roads began.

The railroads made it first. In 1868, the ambitious San Francisco & Humboldt Bay Railroad was organized. It was headed by Asbury Harpending, a "boy wonder" who arrived in California a decade earlier at the age of 16. Now he counted his wealth in millions. But flamboyant Harpending overreached himself. He was blocked by the ruthless "Big Four" of the Central Pacific (Stanford, Huntington, Hopkins, Crocker) and had to sell out. Ironmonger Peter Donahue owned the franchise awhile and renamed the road the San Francisco & North Pacific. He launched rails north from Donahue's Landing, in the marshes east of Petaluma. They had reached Cloverdale by 1872, and deep water at Tiburon. A rival line, Milton S. Latham's narrow-gauge North Pacific Coast, went up to the Russian River and down to Sausalito.

At the north end, the Eel River & Eureka Railroad opened a 25-mile stretch from Eureka to Hydesville, on the Van Duzen River, in 1884. But a great gap yawned between the various lines, punctuated by gorges and torrents.

Peter Donahue's son Mervyn pushed the railhead to Ukiah in 1889, where he swooned from conviviality while pounding in the traditional gold spike. Jovial Mervyn died the next year and left the job of finishing the road to A. W. Foster, a foxy San Rafael financier. Outmaneuvering Eastern moneymen, Foster organized the California Northwestern Railroad Co.

In between came—and perished—a score of smaller railway ventures, including the exotic Sonoma Valley Prismoidal, a sort of primitive monorail running for three miles on a continuous wooden pyramid, from tidewater toward Sonoma.

A classic donnybrook developed between Foster's California Northwestern and the electric Petaluma & Santa Rosa over access to Santa Rosa across CNW tracks. A day-long battle, featuring steam hoses and locomotive battering rams, ended on March 1, 1905, in victory for the electric railway.

Clearing a slide at Scotia Bluffs, early 1900's. Recently shoring and undercutting stabilized this mighty mobile cliff, but the Eel River destroyed the tracks in an epic flood in 1964.

154

The southern railhead was now at Sherwood, north of Willits. But between Sherwood and Shiveley, on the Lower Eel River, there remained a 100-mile no-man's-land through the deep Eel River canyon. Engineers calculated a rail line would cost $150,000 a mile to build. (They were close. It averaged—eventually—$25 a foot.) Eurekans began to feel they were doomed forever to ride the stage to Willits.

In the early 1900's high finance intervened. The upstart Santa Fe had reached Oakland, and its president, Edward Payson Ripley, was eyeing the untapped redwood forests for freight revenue. Quietly Santa Fe bought up the Eel River & Eureka, plus its feeder lines, and Ripley now approached Foster to purchase the California Northwestern.

He was a few days late. Crafty E. H. Harriman, controlling genius of the Southern Pacific (as the Central Pacific was now called), already had a commitment from Foster. In retaliation Ripley merged the roads up north under the name of the San Francisco & North Western, and the Santa Fe "cross" went up in Eureka. Survey parties scurried up the Eel River and into Lake and Napa counties to scout a Santa Fe connection with the Oakland trackage.

But eventually both Harriman and Ripley had to recognize the obstacles and expenses involved in conquering the Eel. Finally they decided the traffic wouldn't warrant two lines. On November 26, 1906, they joined to form the Northwestern Pacific Railroad Company, and when prosperity resumed after the Panic of 1907, construction began.

Six locomotives were ferried to Eureka. Construction crews began pushing south from Shiveley, north from Longvale and Dos Rios (past which no highway ventures to this day). Thirty tunnels were drilled, mostly by hand. Landslides often sent the new-laid tracks plummeting down into the Eel—a nightly occurrence in one area—and the Eel might rise 30 feet in a few hours to wipe out another roadbed.

Against all odds, the job was done in 1914. On October 14, Superintendent W. S. Palmer drove the final spike near Alderpoint, where the road's great 1,117-foot bridge spans the Eel. Boulders fell on the tracks as the train proceeded to Eureka. The town that had waited half a century had to wait awhile longer for its jamboree. On July 1, 1915, regular service began between Sausalito and Trinidad.

Living in San Francisco after a storybook career, boy-wonder Asbury Harpending, 75, was the last survivor of those who had laid the foundations for the Northwestern Pacific.

The road has not been an unqualified success. Its right-of-way is reputed to be the most expensive to maintain of any on earth—$10,000 a mile per year versus a national average of $4,000. Southern Pacific bought out Santa Fe in 1929, and the interurban commuter system in Marin was abandoned in 1941 after the Golden Gate Bridge brought competition for traffic.

Though trackside residents depend heavily on NWP, passenger revenues have declined steadily, and service was cut to thrice weekly in 1956. Now passengers ride only between Willits and Eureka, on a single self-propelled Budd car. Traffic south of San Rafael ceased altogether in 1962 after a fire which caved in the Puerto Suelo Tunnel. The floods of 1964 washed out 100 miles of track and three bridges, clogged a dozen tunnels. Ten million dollars and six months were needed for repairs.

Still freight continues profitable in the valley of the Eel, and for passengers there is an unmatched scenic treat through redwoods and down wild and lonesome canyons.

Island Mountain Tunnel, one of 22 remaining on the Willits-Eureka run, as backdrop for Northwestern Pacific Railroad's Budd car. Below is the swift Main Fork of the Eel, which has been known to rise almost 100 feet in a night's storm. In Christmas week, 1964, it did just that, and this bridge was swept away.

Highway Breakthrough

As the railroad thrust northward it encouraged road construction radiating out from each successive railhead. Logging roads had begun to extend north and south from Eureka, and as the towns of Willits, Ukiah, Cloverdale, Healdsburg, Santa Rosa, Petaluma, and San Rafael grew, each pushed out roads until all were connected.

As with the railroad, a formidable gap continued to exist in the valley of the Eel. The first efforts from the Eureka side tended to avoid the canyon's sheer walls, dense forests, and swiftly rising waters. Those early roads followed cattle trails out to the Coast past Cape Mendocino and down the Mattole River, or east and south through Kneeland Prairie, Bridgeville, Blocksburg, and Alderpoint. Here the route straddled the ridge tops before descending in steep corkscrews to the canyons north of Laytonville.

As late as 1911, this stretch over 4,600-foot Bell Springs Mountain, known as the Mail Ridge Road, was impassable for automobiles in any except the driest weather. It took bold motorists three full days to drive to Dyerville from San Francisco Bay, and most of a fourth day to reach Eureka. Broken springs and axles, burst tires and radiators were normal.

In January, 1912, Harvey M. Harper, who had just obtained the Ford agency in Eureka, began the perilous journey north with his family in a Model T touring car. On the hillsides north of Willits, Mrs. Harper was "delegated the dubious honor of holding the Ford to the incline with a rope so it would not slide off into the river below." Harper walked ahead and shoveled a muddy path for the wheels. When, after numerous halts for repairs, the Harpers drove into Bridgeville, the townsfolk were astonished, "for it was generally believed that no automobile could make that trip." The voyagers reached Eureka on February 25, and by the end of September, Harvey Harper had sold 32 Fords.

The first roads were private or at best county projects, meagerly engineered and financed. Not until 1910, when California authorized its first highway bonds, did any sizable highway funds become available. And because the state managed to sell only about a quarter of the first issue of $18 million, the Redwood Empire counties had to subscribe their own money to get the earth moving. First projects were grading a road from Hopland to the south Mendocino County line, and paving 14 miles from Healdsburg to Santa Rosa.

By 1914, surveys had been made or were under way on 111 miles of road between Sausalito and Crescent City, almost a third of the 381 miles. Survey crews could not use the main fork of the Eel, since the railroad had preempted it, so they tried the longer but less steep-sided South Fork.

Though work was hampered by lack of cash, it proceeded steadily. In 1916 the *California Highway Bulletin* reported: "It is doubtful whether the completion of any stretch of road in the State is looked forward to with more eagerness than the gap between Cummings and the Humboldt County line, a distance of 29.3 miles. [It] means the elimination of 2686 feet of heavy grades, the erection of several bridges. The country traversed is in a virgin state, for the most part devoid of wagon roads or even passable trails. The scenery is unsurpassed in California, and the redwood forests, river views and picturesque ruggedness will be a revelation to the tourist."

Of the old Bell Springs route, the *Bulletin* noted "after the first rains come [in October] this road is impassable for motor vehicles, and even for horse-drawn vehicles. When snow storms set in, transportation is limited to saddle and pack animals."

Much of the new road was built by convict labor, from state prison camps. These "trusties" were permitted, under a law of 1915, to receive a dollar a day in pay and two days' "time" was credited for each day worked. Even during World War I, when shortages of manpower and material stopped roadwork in many states, California was able to continue its construction, using these men. On the Redwood Highway, the program ultimately expanded to several camps of 125 prisoners each, working year round, every day but Sunday, in snow and rain up to 70 inches a year.

In a recent series of articles for *California Highways & Public Works* Magazine, John Robinson credits convict labor for much of the speed with which the Redwood Highway, once undertaken, got built.

"By 1920," Robinson points out, "there was a passable road between Sausalito and Eureka," though as late as 1925, long stretches still were unpaved.

By 1930, the entire highway had been "improved" to standards set before World War I. But this included narrow, curving alignments and timber bridges. During the 1930's, 1940's, and up to the present time, more than $600 million has been spent updating the Redwood Highway to the age of 65-mile-an-hour speed limits and 20-ton trucks.

Above: *"The Devil's Elbow", motorists called this hairpin curve on the Fruitland Grade, where the Mail Ridge Road dropped off in its descent to McCann, on the main fork of the Eel River. Photo made about 1912. Cars making turn had to back up to negotiate it.* Left: *Mired in the redwoods. The driver of this 1913 Overland pauses to drink from a water bag, standard equipment for travelers even in rain forests.*

Below: *Bell Springs Mountain route, or Mail Ridge Road, with car (distant center), about 1910, at elevation of 4,000 feet. From 1870's until about 1920, this was the only way to get from Willits to Eureka, by auto. It still can be traveled in good weather.* Above: *This was the Redwood Highway through Garberville, in 1914. Garberville, in southern Humboldt County, is a motel and restaurant center today.*

Bogged down near Healdsburg in 1914.
Construction continued despite mishaps like
these. A freeway replaced older roads here
in 1963.

Redwood Highway segments were
subject to frequent washouts in
bad weather. This one on
Rattlesnake Grade was repaired
temporarily with local logs.

Double-arch 210-foot bridge, with trusses made
of redwood, spans Rock Creek in northern
Mendocino County, in 1916. Tower at right
supported lines carrying materials into position.
Bridge was replaced by concrete in the 1930's.

By the 1930's it was possible to drive for many miles over paved roads through the redwood forests. Scene is in southern Humboldt County about 1939.

How They Got the Roads

After the state tacitly assumed responsibility for major highways in 1910, California's road-fund history became one of regional tugs-of-war.

In the mid-1920's, the state's total highway fund was still only $25 million a year, and the legislature allocated the slices where the votes were. This restricted the slimly populated Redwood Empire counties to a negligible share of the highway cash.

Recognizing that good roads were the key to development of the North Coastal region, especially with the upsurge in automobile ownership after World War I, some of the more farsighted "poison-oakers" (as upcountry folks are called) decided to unite to achieve the political strength they required.

In 1921, they formed the Redwood Highway Association, superseded (and broadened in scope) in 1925 by the Redwood Empire Association. It aimed to develop the region as a whole through better roads. Clyde Edmonson, bus-firm executive, became general manager and directed lobbying efforts in Sacramento and work-together programs for the membership. Nine counties as a unit made the mark no single county could, and state money began flowing north.

The Redwood Empire Association (REA) deserves credit for much of the acceleration in highway construction. Almost a billion dollars' worth of roads, plus the Golden Gate Bridge, have been built with REA backing. The lucrative tourist industry has grown steadily.

Now an estimated five million travelers visit the Redwood Empire each year. More than two million are counted at the Humboldt Redwood State Parks alone.

Under REA's prodding, tourism is becoming the region's "second industry," supplying outside dollars to augment lumbering payrolls.

Left: *Motorists of the 1960's have a choice: they can take almost 30 miles of fast freeway through southern Humboldt County's magnificent redwood stands, or mosey a slightly longer distance over a parallel scenic route called The Avenue of the Giants. The latter permits leisurely viewing, undisturbed by trucks or through traffic. Above is one of the first legs of the Redwood Freeway, opened in 1958. Below: Light and shadow form a pattern on the new Redwood Freeway near Myers Flat in southern Humboldt County. This fast highway ultimately will extend more than 50 miles. It parallels the scenic Avenue of the Giants, where trees may be viewed and photographed under ideal conditions. The "Avenue" actually is the old two-lane Highway 101, maintained for redwood appreciators.*

Big Tree Country:
First Probers North

What human being first saw the fog-piercing redwood spires on the lower Eel, the gold-strewn beaches below the Klamath?

Undoubtedly a prehistoric man who shaped flint arrowheads and worshipped ghosts. We sense his dim presence in the eternal forests and uncover his crude artifacts. Did he arrive, or evolve?

Persistent legends insist the first Outlanders were Chinese, appearing two centuries before the Christian era. The journal of a Celestial shipmaster, Hee-li, was found in the archives of Shensi, by an American missionary in 1890. This sailor wrote that in 217 B.C., his vessel being turned eastward by a storm, he sailed in the wrong direction for four months, due to a cockroach which wedged itself under the compass needle. Then, said Hee-li, he came upon a wild wooded shore. He explored awhile, found a great inland harbor [San Francisco Bay?] which he called Hong-Tsi. Eventually, he extracted the cockroach, and turned for home.

Skeptical nautical critics point out that China didn't invent the compass until about the fifth century A.D., when a boatload of Buddhist monks reputedly made the trip. Whatever the value of these stories, it is certain that junks frequently were blown into the Pacific. Thus the possibility exists that these Chinese proved equal to Leif Ericson. The first precisely recorded explorations are Spanish, and the records are sparse. By order of Hernan Cortez, conqueror and viceroy of Mexico, Captain Juan Rodriguez Cabrillo sailed north in 1542, seeking a passage around the top of the continent. Groping through fogs and storms, he sighted a mountainous headland above the 40th Parallel and named it Cape of Perils. Sixty years later another Spaniard, Sebastián Vizcaino, rechristened it Cape Mendocino in honor of the viceroy, Antonio de Mendoza.

In the years after 1565 Spain's glittering Manila galleons, sailing east for Acapulco, used Cape Mendocino as a landfall. It was a welcome sight, for the Manila-to-Mexico crossing, against winds and currents, was deemed the "longest and most dreadful of any in the world," consuming six or eight months and often the lives of many crewmen. Once a year, these stately treasure ships coasted south past the redwood cliffs. Sometimes the rendezvous was fatal—gales blew the galleons onto shore and pounded them into splinters. From 1565 to 1815, thirty Manila ships were lost on the crossing. Indian lore says at least one cargo of gold and jewels was salvaged by the Mattole tribes and now lies hidden in a secret cave under King Peak.

The first Europeans to come ashore alive may have been the Spanish navigators Bruno de Heceta and Juan de Bodega, on June 11, 1775. Since it was Trinity Sunday, their chaplain, Father Campa, celebrated Mass on Trinidad Head, north of present-day Eureka. The bay and the headland were named for the holy day, and a rude cross was placed to commemorate the first Christian services held on the north coast. In 1793, Captain George Vancouver, an inquisitive British seaman, visited Trinidad and noted the name of King Charles III inscribed in the crumbling wood. (A granite monument marks the site today.)

Zoomorph—that's the scientific name for this animal-shaped slate artifact, uncovered a few years ago on Gunther Island in Humboldt Bay, and now treasured with three similar pieces in Eureka's Clarke Museum. These stones are believed to be unique, fashioned by prehistoric tribes, perhaps for worship. In Eskimo territory, two thousand miles north, they are known as "slave killers."

162

*Galleons' grave? Rocky indentation in the coast south of Cape Mendocino,
in Humboldt County, may have been scene of shipwrecks when
Spain's annual Manila galleon made her last landfall in a storm.*

For a long time visitors came only by sea. In 1805–1806 otter skins tempted a handful of skippers into this part of the Pacific. The Yankee brig *O'Cain* under Captain Jonathan Winship, eased into Trinidad Bay early, with a complement of Aleut fur hunters. *O'Cain* and Winship were back the following summer, and the captain told his employer, the Russian-American Company, that he'd sailed into a much larger harbor to the south, which he named Rezanof. This may have been Humboldt Bay, but if so its turbulent entrance repelled other mariners, and they continued to anchor at Trinidad.

In 1828 came the first overland visitor, Jedediah Strong Smith, mountain man and fur trader. Expelled from California by the Mexican authorities, Smith worked his way up the Valley of the Sacramento, heading for the Hudson's Bay settlements in Oregon. But he was blocked by the Cascades, so he swerved west into the Coast Ranges, driving 300 half-wild horses and mules intended for sale in the Rockies. Smith found the Hay Fork of the Trinity River somewhere near Wildwood, followed it to the main fork, then to its confluence with the Klamath.

Smith's arduous journey to the Pacific is preserved in his comrades' journals. Sometimes the party made only a mile a day. Animals tumbled into the wild gorges. Armed Indians harassed the party constantly, shooting the horses which they mistook for a new kind of elk. Near the mouth of the Klamath, creeping fearfully through dense June fog the Americans almost had to turn back, so terrible was the terrain. Finally a path was found, and ultimately they reached the sea. Driving the stock along the beaches, sometimes in the surf, Smith and his fellow-trappers rested a few days on the site of today's Crescent City.

Then they pushed on into Oregon. There the Umpqua Indians massacred all except Smith and three companions. Broken and exhausted, the courageous pathfinder turned east for the last time. He was killed three years later by Comanches on the Cimarron River.

Jed Smith is as remarkable for his piety and his love of nature as for his adventurous spirit. His importance rests on a dozen amazing achievements. He blazed the southern and central routes to the Pacific, the Oregon-California trail, and first breached the Sierra Nevada. Smith River and a majestic redwood park in Del Norte County are his memorials.

News traveled slowly in Jed Smith's day, and his coastal discoveries caused little stir. Ewing Young, another roaming trapper, struggled north to Oregon from Fort Ross in 1836, in search of beaver, but they proved scarce. Michael Laframboise, a French *voyageur* who reputedly had an Indian wife in every village, also found few furs on a push into the King Range, behind Cape Mendocino. Indeed, what beaver would have the temerity to challenge a redwood?

163

*Dr. Josiah Gregg,
from a contemporary sketch.*

Gold fever hastened the tempo of overland travel. Major Pierson B. Reading, who had discovered the Trinity River a few years earlier, found "color" on its headwaters in July, 1848, only six months after Jim Marshall's epochal strike at Coloma. San Francisco came alive with hungry Argonauts. Though some traced Reading's trail up the Sacramento, many took the shorter sea route to Trinidad Bay, intending to cut overland to the diggings.

Before they could get under way, another party came out to the Coast from the Trinity mines. It was led by Dr. Josiah Gregg, physician and author, toiling west from Rich Bar in November rain and snow. Gregg and his seven compatriots were hunting for the "lost harbor," variously called Rezanof, Trinity Bay, or (in Indian) Qualawaloo. They believed it would make their fortunes.

After a month's battle, the Gregg party reached the sea south of Trinidad. Here the scholarly Gregg hauled out navigational instruments and tried to take his bearings. "Come along," curtly ordered the others. At a swift river, north of present Arcata, he stopped again and asked help to measure a tremendous tree, 21 feet thick. This delay provoked an explosion among the majority, hurrying to find civilization and stake out land claims. A row developed between the scientist and his land-hungry companions. Thus the Mad River got its name.

The breach widened as Gregg's party skirted a saltwater bay. Was this the lost harbor? Perhaps, but food was running out and nobody had time to make sure. The group pressed southward. On December 29, at the junction of the Eel and Van Duzen rivers, the party split. Testy L. K. Wood led one faction down the Coast and ultimately to Santa Rosa, though not before Wood was badly mauled by a grizzly bear. Gregg's reduced band slogged down the muddy Eel (so named because Indians swapped them a mess of eels for a broken frypan) and pushed eastward to Clear Lake. Weakened by strife and hunger, Josiah Gregg slipped from his horse and died. His brother hinted he may have been slain or at least abandoned by the others. His grave, and his diaries, have never been found.

The remainder of Gregg's party made their way to San Francisco. Their news caused fresh excitement. California had just been admitted to the Union, and the north quarter of the state had been split into two counties: Shasta on the east, Trinity on the west. With the Trinity mining boom at its height, merchants and land speculators could see potential profits in a new seaport at the lost harbor.

Several companies were formed to seize the opportunity. In late March, 1850, no less than 11 vessels weighed anchor in San Francisco, bound for the Bay of Trinity, or was it Qualawaloo?

First at the scene was *Laura Virginia*, captained by Douglas Ottinger; her second mate was Hans Henry Buhne. From her masthead the lookout could see the lost bay, but breakers hid the entrance. Meantime Mormon millionaire Sam Brannan's bark *General Morgan* anchored to the south, off the Eel River, where Sam put a party ashore. *James R. Whiting* and *Isabel* landed men at Trinidad, up north, and started claiming land. Lewis K. Wood was guiding the Union Company north by land. Brannan's Mendocino Company, headed by James Talbot Ryan, started dragging a whaleboat around Table Bluff, sweating hard to be the first into the bay.

That honor probably fell to a boatload under Hans Henry Buhne, though precise dates are uncertain. On April 9, Buhne, with other members of the *Laura Virginia* party, squeezed over the harbor bar, landing south of the present city of Eureka. Ryan's boat plopped in, perhaps a day later; and Wood's footsore group came up a little after that. The rival parties argued over boundaries for a while, then on May 13 a pact was signed, giving Wood's Union Company full rights to the region north of the bay, Ryan's group most of the eastern shore.

Ryan, a cultured Irishman, drew on his Greek to name the new town. He called it *Eureka,* "I have found it." This motto is echoed on the Great Seal of California, though in this case it refers to Marshall's gold.

The bay was named for Baron Alexander von Humboldt; tradition says the choice was Ottinger's, *Laura Virginia*'s skipper, who admired the German naturalist. Von Humboldt never saw his bay, though the proud Eurekans invited him out, and even offered to give him a city lot if he would come.

It might have been worth the trip—within three years Eureka had grown to a prosperous port of 2,000 people, where 100 ships called.

Mule pack-train for the Trinity mines loads for A. Brizard Company at the John Preston ranch, on Alliance Road, north of present Arcata. The town was then called Union and was laid out in corral-shaped segments, to accommodate the freighting industry, which centered here. Ericson photo.

Redskins of the Redwoods

How did the Original Settlers view their new neighbors, rushing to fill a vacuum with 1850-style civilization?

Father Campa records that the redwood Indians looked upon navigator Heceta's men as gods. Disciplined, or perhaps just squeamish, the Spaniards left the Indians' squaws alone. Their Yankee successors were less godlike.

There were several ethnic varieties of Redwood Indians. The main tribes were the Kiruk, or up-rivers; the Yurok, down-river; and the Hoopa, who lived around the confluence of the Klamath and the Trinity.

Each culture had its distinct characteristics and language: it was said a man could wander from one tribe to the next and never hear the same tongue twice.

For the Kiruk, the Center of the World was near their sacred village of Ishipishi, on the Klamath near the mouth of the Salmon, under the great Ridge Up Which Go the Souls of the Dead. So it had been since the world was formed by Ik-hareya, the Race Preceding Men. Ik-hareya sent the salmon upriver each spring, and the Kiruk, Yurok, and Hoopa all celebrated the demigods' gift with dances and ceremonies. Buttressed by traditional myths, in which animals spoke in parables, their children honored their parents, and the tribes lived in relative peace.

Of all California's 117 tribal cultures, the Kiruk, Yurok, and Hoopa stayed untouched the longest. The Spaniards were ignorant of their river valleys. But in 1850, after discovery of gold on the Trinity, gun-toting miners broke into the Upper Klamath and burned two sacred villages. The Indians retaliated, and the years until the end of the Civil War were scarred with bipartisan massacres. Not until about 1870 did the Original Settlers bow to superior firepower.

"Delia," a Lake Earl (Del Norte) Indian, models tribal dress, including shell beads, grass skirt, and basket cap, for pioneer photographer A. W. Ericson. Indian women were modest, possessed great endurance. When married, they were tattooed with three vertical lines on their chins.

166

Wearing full regalia for the Jump Dance, redwood braves are photographed by Ericson, circa 1893. Headdresses are made from the scalps of redheaded woodpeckers, baskets contain loose grain to ensure a good harvest. Necklaces are dentalium shells, principal measure of wealth among the money-conscious Yuroks. Dentalium—"little tusks"—were painstakingly gathered by other tribes underwater at Cape Flattery, 800 miles to the north, and were valued according to size. One string of the largest shells would pay for a wife, or a slave. A warrior might be fined five smaller strings for fathering a bastard, fifteen for a murder.

Of California's 200,000 Indians who hunted, fished, and went their dignified ways before the white men came, only 15,500 were alive by 1900. The redwood tribes were luckier than most. In 1864, a troubled government established the Hoopa Reservation astride the Trinity in central Humboldt County. Today it is the only active agency in Northern California, administering several thousand acres for the benefit of about 3,000 Indians. In 1961, for example, nearly $1 million was distributed to 1,034 Hoopas, the proceeds of timber sales on their ancestral lands. Other profits are kept in trust to educate younger members of the tribe.

The Hoopa and their neighbors now blend in almost totally with twentieth-century California: they wear store-bought clothes and work in the woods. Occasionally Abraham Jack, Rudolph Socktish, or some other "leader" who has preserved the tradition, will call for the Brush Dance, the Jump Dance, or the White Deerskin ceremony. Then, where no white man can see, the ancient ritual is revived, the bountiful harvest invoked, the salmon god propitiated.

But one old Kiruk whispered not long ago, just before she died:

"Yis-ara-to-peen"—new people are taking over.

167

In horn headdresses, carrying big obsidian skin-scrapers, Yurok men pose for Ericson before their White Deer Dance. Object of the ceremony was to promote good hunting. In background are deer heads and skins on sticks, examples of which can be seen today in Eureka's Clarke Museum. These Indians also played a villainous form of hockey called the Stick Game, and gambled with tufts of grass. Ericson's are the only photos of actual dances of the 1890's.

On the Klamath, a Yurok transports his
household in a redwood dugout 50 years ago.
Since felling a redwood was too ambitious for
the Indians, they collected driftwood logs,
burned and scraped them into boat shape. This
tribe required its members to give free ferry
service to travelers.

Sam Grant at Eureka

"Scalawags and plunderers" infiltrated the Humboldt country behind the first exploration companies. In ragged beards and buckskins, the dregs of goldfields and docks spread inland, hungry for land and gold.

To these white savages, Indians were a nuisance and an obstacle. "Get out of the way, you damned Digger," the ruffians ordered. An eyewitness wrote in the Humboldt *Times:* "If [the Indians] resisted, they were killed, butchered, shot down with as little hesitation as wolves and coyotes."

At first, redskin retaliation was swift. Offending palefaces were slain and burned in their canyon outposts. Inevitably, so were decent settlers, for the outraged redmen couldn't distinguish. For years, it was unsafe to venture outside the towns—the Indians had picked up the custom of murder. Even this was turned to profit by criminal whites: more than one rancher was killed by Indian renegades, hired by claim jumpers who coveted the rancher's land.

Fort Humboldt, as it appeared to the photographer Vansant in the 1860's, after Captain Ulysses S. Grant had departed with his "first" Army career in shards. Second cottage from left reportedly was Grant's quarters; two-story buildings are enlisted barracks. Fort was abandoned in 1870, soon tumbled down. Only one building, the hospital (right), survives. State of California now preserves site as a historic monument, is slowly reconstructing Fort Humboldt as a reminder of days when it was America's farthest-west outpost.

Fort Humboldt, near Eureka,
Where General Grant, then Captain, was stationed in 1853-4. indicates Grant's quarters.

*Sunset, fishing boat at anchor;
Little River on the Mendocino Coast.
Through pines from Little River Inn.*

*Marin County Civic Center,
designed by Frank Lloyd Wright.*

Ulysses S. Grant as a young officer, 1843.

Anarchy brought Federal intervention. In January, 1853, the government dispatched Brevet Lieutenant Colonel Robert C. Buchanan to establish a base of action at Eureka. With five officers and 82 men of the U.S. 4th Infantry, Colonel Buchanan sailed from Benicia. Soon his troops were digging trenches and raising barracks on a bluff overlooking the harbor. They called their stronghold Fort Humboldt. Its 640 acres Buchanan deemed sufficient "to secure the woodlands and gardens and keep off the groggeries."

Buchanan's adjutant was Lieutenant George Crook, who was to become a famous Indian fighter. In his journal, Crook shows little liking for his commanding officer. He considered him bull-headed, a button-inspector.

In October, Lieutenant Crook was sent east to Fort Jones, near Yreka. Later that month there came to Fort Humboldt from Vancouver, Washington, one Ulysses S. Grant, newly promoted captain, to assume command of F Company. "Sam" Grant had won a reputation in the Mexican War, but now he was bucking ebb tide. He had been forced to leave his wife, Julia, who was expecting their second child, at home in Ohio. He had no resources besides his Army pay; advancement seemed at an end. Fort Humboldt and Indian-chasing meant to Grant the grave of his ambition.

There was another complication. Grant had sown the seed of a drinking reputation at a succession of dreary postwar Army posts. In remote, fogbound Fort Humboldt, this image came to flower. The captain spent off-duty hours slouching, stubble-chinned, around the whiskey barrel in Ryan's Store. The story goes that one night Grant primed himself into a merry mood, hitched three buggies in tandem, and rollicked in this fashion back to the fort. Colonel Buchanan got wind of it. He berated Grant, and forced him to sign an undated letter of resignation. Though boozing was an accepted frontier pastime, Buchanan clearly was not going to tolerate it in this unpromising captain.

In April, 1854, brooding and inactivity again took their toll. Captain Grant was observed weaving unsteadily at the pay table. Colonel Buchanan swung the ax. The letter of resignation went forward, without explanation, to take effect July 21. Long before that Sam Grant was en route to San Francisco, from thence to Ohio and civilian life. Six years of seedy storekeeping lay ahead, before chance and the Civil War called him back to command a regiment of Illinois Volunteers.

The day he left Eureka, Captain Grant told Post Surgeon Jonathan Clark: "My day will come, they will hear from me yet." If Dr. Clark discerned signs of a future Army commander and President in his friend's troubled face, he failed to report it.

Grant's own life story, written on his deathbed, gives only one line to those five dismal months at Fort Humboldt. Yet something in the redwood frontier called to his stubborn soul: he says he would have liked to make his home there.

171

Mr. Ryan Names His Town

In Washington to settle Indian War claims, James Talbot Ryan was introduced by Senator McDougall to President Lincoln in these terms:

"Mr. President, this is General Ryan, a loyal friend and neighbor, who can build a vessel and sail it, an engine and run it, a cathedral and preach in it, and make a better stump speech, Mr. President, than either of us."

Abraham Lincoln's reply is lost, but James Talbot Ryan unquestionably was a man of parts. One historian calls him the founder of Eureka, and a leader to whom residents of the region "are more largely indebted than to any other man."

Irish by birth, he was a descendant of the Talbots, earls of Shrewsbury. In Boston he was a successful contractor before he sailed for the goldfields. It was Ryan who led the *General Morgan* whaleboat across the sands in 1850. That May, he returned to lay out the town of Eureka with a homemade transit. And he wasted no time in convincing the Indians he was trustworthy. They called him *Mowema*, the Conciliator.

In San Francisco, Ryan bought the steamer *Santa Clara* and signed a partnership with James Duff. They loaded her deck with sawmill machinery and headed for Humboldt Bay. Crossing Humboldt Bar, the mill washed overside. So Ryan anchored and had a canal dug onshore, heading inland. Then he got up a full head of steam and drove *Santa Clara* up the canal onto the beach. There he harnessed the ship's engines and converted her to a sawmill. This was in February, 1852, and Ryan was anxious to provide San Francisco with the lumber she needed.

Soon Ryan & Duff were sawing 80,000 feet a day—pine and fir, since the mighty redwoods were inland and too monstrous to handle. In June the partners loaded their first cargo on the brig *Clifford* and dispatched her southward. But she grounded and broke apart crossing the bar. A few days later they sent off the bark *Cornwallis*, only to see her meet the same fate. Finally in despair Ryan persuaded Hans Henry Buhne to take out a third cargo in the bark *Home*. On July 4 Buhne set sail. But the jinx held, and *Home* was driven ashore on the south spit.

Despite these triple blows, and the loss of a mill by fire, Ryan persisted. Finally the firm knew success. Friends said nothing daunted this man, not even the wilderness. When Eureka consisted of only a few mills and 20 frame houses, Ryan's home was the finest of all, his table the most hospitable, his wife the most accomplished and charming. During Sam Grant's lonely stay at Fort Humboldt, the two men became friends. The lumber king placed at Grant's disposal his favorite horse Eclipse, and the captain pronounced the mount "finest west of the Rockies."

James Ryan went on to serve in the State Senate, and to command the militia of Northern California with the rank of brigadier general. During his visit to Washington, he designed a hydraulic revolving iron fort for harbor defense, and he built the ironclad monitor *Comanche* in a San Francisco shipyard.

Said a noted judge: "Wherever you put him, he always led."

James Talbot Ryan, founder of Eureka.

Eureka in 1864, showing G Street from Third to Fourth; beyond rises the forest.

Pioneer photographer Augustus W. Ericson, in holiday garb for the Fourth of July, 1877, stands in the doorway of his stationery shop and telegraph office opposite the Plaza in Arcata. A Swede who worked first in the woods and mills, Ericson took up wet-plate photography as a hobby, made his first prints by sunlight, manufactured his own photo paper. He traveled around the redwood country making pictures of logging, ships, railroads, and Indians, usually with an 8 x 10-inch box camera. His studies of Indian ceremonies (preceding pages) are considered unique. Ericson died at 79 in 1927. Examples of his work in this book are used by permission of his daughter, Mrs. Percy Bryan. A. W. Ericson in later years published photo albums from his fine glass-plate negatives, and these received nationwide circulation.

"The Chinese Must Go"

"The Chinese must go," was demagogue Dennis Kearney's slogan in San Francisco in the 1870's. Though Kearney's campaign to free the white worker from Oriental competition finally failed, traces of resentment against the industrious Chinese lingered in many a California town.

Eureka's Chinese were as busy and self-contained as any other colony on the Coast. They operated laundries and shops, toiled as servants to earn enough to send home for a wife, or to be sent home to die. They also settled their obscure face-saving differences among themselves. In 1885 this propensity was the Eureka Chinese's undoing.

A tong war, so-called, broke out in waterfront Chinatown on February 13. A Eureka city councilman, David Kendal, heard shooting. He stepped down into Chinatown to investigate, and was felled by a stray bullet.

A town meeting was called. Next day Chinatown was evacuated at gunpoint, and 480 pigtailed exiles were loaded aboard ships and sent off to San Francisco. Ninety miles north at Crescent City, the local burghers thought Kendal's death a sufficient excuse to ship out their Celestial colony, too.

In all of Humboldt County only one Chinese—a cook—was permitted to stay, and only because he was vouched for by his employer on remote Redwood Creek. It was years before any Oriental dared show his face in Eureka.

Sequoia Sempervirens *as the first Americans saw them, captured on*
glass by A. W. Ericson. Ericson's young son is in the buggy.

Ridge after ridge of redwoods, on the Klamath
River, looking northeast. Morning mist rises
from the damp forest. This was remarked
by the earliest adventurers.

Redwood Discovery

Riding north with the Portola Expedition in 1769, Fray Juan Crespi was the first to sight "very high trees of a red color, not known to us." This was on October 10, in the low hills northeast of today's Watsonville. Father Crespi was amazed by the trees' abundance and size, adding that "because none of the expedition recognizes them, they are named red wood [*palo colorado*] from their color."

Seven years later, as the Anza Expedition paused south of San Francisco Bay, Fray Pedro Font noted in his journal, "a few trees they call redwood, . . . very useful for its timber, for it is very straight and tall . . ." One of the redwoods Father Font observed survives today in Palo Alto, to which it gave its name; it also is depicted on the seal of nearby Stanford University.

Palo colorado or redwood, it was all one to the Down Easters. The Men of Maine came to woo fortune the way they knew best, now that California gold had begun to tarnish. In the Santa Cruz mountains, in the Oakland hills, beside the rivers of Sonoma, Americans were building sawmills. Steam and steel helped overcome their awe of the massive trees. They felled them Maine-style, sawed them up for studs and shingles, for fences and furniture, the raw materials to build a state.

Dense stand of coast redwoods beside Bull Creek in Humboldt County. Taller and more graceful, these trees lack the girth and age of their cousins of the Sierra, Sequoia Gigantea. *The coastal specimens thrive only in a foggy belt extending from Oregon's Chetco River south to Salmon Creek, in Monterey County.*

Waste in the Woods

James Talbot Ryan was not quite the first to build a sawmill on Humboldt Bay. Martin White and James Eddy did that in September, 1850, four months after the exploration parties arrived. For a while the settlers actually imported lumber!

White & Eddy's mill, the Taupoos, sat near what is now Second and M streets, Eureka. It failed within the year. So did a few more, leaving Ryan and Duff to run the first successful enterprise, in their ship on the beach between D and E.

By 1854, nine mills were sawing fir and pine on Humboldt Bay. But not redwood. Everyone suspected profits lay in the big trees, but nobody cared to tackle 400 tons of tree. Finally in 1856 a New Brunswicker, William Carson, took the plunge. Using a leased mill, Carson sawed and shipped the first redwood lumber across Humboldt Bar. In no time, redwood was the rage in San Francisco. Its elegant color and its rot-resistance commanded premium prices. By 1863, Carson had joined forces with John Dolbeer, and their firm name would last well into the next century.

In 1881 Humboldt County supported 22 sawmills. Such activity required plenty of raw materials and vast tracts of timber. Eager capitalists in San Francisco and New York envisioned fortunes if their band saws could be assured a supply. Like blinders on a house detective, the U.S. Homestead Act provided that assurance.

Stephen D. Puter, self-confessed bagman for the land pirates, told how. As a seaport, Eureka had a wealth of idle sailors. Puter would take gangs of them to the local government land office, there have each file homestead claims on 160 acres of choice forest. The mariner received $50 for his claim, then Puter redeemed it to a waiting timber corporation. The land was resold to an operating company, which began to cut trees and saw logs. Thus everyone profited, and thousands of acres of prime public land were captured by the big combines. Peter B. Kyne's novel *Valley of the Giants* draws on this marauding as a base for its fiction.

Six-foot undercut and not halfway through the tree. A visitor poses to give the scale.

Felling a big one before 1900. One reporter who witnessed this sight was moved to comment: "When such a tree begins to totter, it gives at first a sharp crack; the cutter labors with his axe usually about fifteen minutes . . . when at last the huge mass begins to go over. Then you may hear one of the grandest sounds of the forest. The fall of a great redwood is startlingly like a prolonged thunder-crash, and is really a terrible sound."

Eventually there was a reckoning. President Cleveland appointed B. F. Bergin as special agent to investigate the frauds. Bergin's findings caused the cancellation of 200 homesteads—60,000 acres of choice timber worth $20,000,000. More than 400 witnesses testified on behalf of the land-grabbers, but Bergin's report held up.

Despite its tribulations, lumber was recognized as Eureka's mainstay. Though profitable ($2 a pound), the pack-train trade with the Trinity mines was never steady enough to sustain a city. And lumber had its bonanzas. Sometimes finished redwood sold for $75 a thousand board-feet in San Francisco. When word of this got back to Eureka, the mills would hum. But they had to be quick. By the time the cargoes reached the market, prices might have dropped to $15, and freight and towage ran more than that. Thus many small mills had a short life.

A bucking crew slices a peeled log into 2½ foot lengths for shingle bolts. Two cuts were considered a good day's work. Ericson photo.

The physical facets of redwood logging bulked immense as the trees. Larger boles were five days' hard work for two experienced choppers. Humboldt woodsmen took pride in their skill and the rough life they led.

Many of them were Bluenoses from Nova Scotia, apprenticed in Maine or Michigan. Most of them were bachelors, inhabiting log huts in the forest, leading a lonely male existence. Their amusement was coming to town on Saturday's logging trains to celebrate, returning with aching skulls on the "empties" next day.

Then they would sharpen their axes and start the woods cycle again.

Seldom were these Bunyans moved to prose or poetry. But it is recorded that, looking at a particularly tall tree, an old logger might sigh:

"She sure makes a big hole in the sky."

Inevitably there was appalling waste and heartbreaking havoc of nature in the early days of redwood logging. The axmen were concerned with getting out the most timber in the least time.

When a 200-foot forest monarch went down, it carried a whole court with it. Because the tree was immense and the wood soft, a bed of lesser trees had to be felled first so it would not splinter when it landed. This operation might consume as much time as the actual chopping, and destroy dozens of trees. Then there was the peeling of the bark, perhaps a foot thick. This and other debris were burned to clear the ground. Said one writer:

"The whole country is a charred, blackened mass. Every living green twig, every vestige of life has been wiped out." But he added: "Redwood reproduces itself from the suckers which spring up around the stump, and the effect of fire evidently makes very little difference, proving the sublime struggle nature makes for reproduction."

It took two undercuts, then a half-day's sawing to bring down this big butt log in the Humboldt woods. From A. W. Ericson's album Among the Redwoods in California.

180

Still the waste from start to finish averaged between one-third to one-half of the forest. Though he never saw the victims himself, Walt Whitman describes the death of one giant in his poem "Song of the Redwood Tree" (1874):

> "With crackling blows of axes, sounding musically, driven by
>   strong arms,
> Riven deep by the sharp tongues of the axes—there in the
>   Redwood forest dense,
> I heard the mighty tree its death-chant chanting. . . .
> You untold life of me . . . ,
> Perennial, hardy life of me, with joys, 'mid rain, and many
>   a summer sun,
> And the white snows, and night, and the wild winds; . . .
> Joys of the life befitting me and brothers mine,
> Our time, our term has come."

Almost 15 feet in diameter, this cross section was shipped by The Pacific Lumber Company as an exhibit to the Chicago World's Fair in 1893. Magnificently bearded, the lumber company's first logging superintendent, Dan Newell, holds the measuring stick.

A mill town in 1895. Scotia, on the Eel River, shortly before The Pacific Lumber Company mill (right, rear) burned on July 3. This unique town still is entirely company owned.

*Seven span of oxen, commonly called
"bulls," tow a big log over a skid road in
the Humboldt woods in this early photo
by A. W. Ericson. To cross steep or boggy
spots, logs were laid crossways and the
load skidded over the improvised highway.
From this evolved the term "Skid Road,"
now usually "Skid Row." to denote a
slum inhabited by downslid alcoholics.
Lumberjacks were hard drinkers.*

*When John Dolbeer invented the steam
donkey engine (right), he revolutionized
logging. Wood crews hauled it around
on skids and the powerful device would
snake logs out in a fraction of the time
needed by "bull teams." This donkey
uses manila line and a side-spool to do
the job. Bobbie-cars (left) were towed
along by the donkey until picked up by
logging locomotives.*

Work halted at Freshwater, north of Eureka, while Ericson's camera caught two Excelsior Lumber trains hauling a notable shipment of redwood. Log markings indicate one chunk was 11 feet, 9 inches in diameter, 18 feet long. Photo probably was in the mid-1890's. Excelsior was bought by The Pacific Lumber Company in 1905.

Fifty-nine pupils and teachers posed for Ericson on this Sempervirens stump at Korbel. Part of the fun of living in the redwood country was making pictures like this to stupefy friends back East. There was considerable skepticism about the redwoods, and one Englishman used mathematics to prove no tree could grow to a height of 300 feet—it would topple from its own weight.

Carson Mansion, Eureka. Now a private club.

William Carson's Redwood Palace

Sparkling under fresh coats of cream-and-spinach paint, the lofty Carson Mansion in Eureka is the very picture of Victorian glory.

Out come cameras and light meters when travelers sight America's most faithfully preserved monument to Gingerbread Gothic.

On an eminence above Humboldt Bay, hard by the mills and wharves that made William Carson wealthy, the mansion preens like a peacock in a barnyard. Its very aloofness undoubtedly helped save it from fires that razed lesser structures.

William Carson came west to mine gold on the Trinity. But he quickly saw that lumber, and lots of it, would be at a premium to build Californian cities. Hardworking and knowledgeable, he went after the materials at hand.

It took strong men, chopping and sawing on platforms 10 feet high, to fell the huge redwoods. It took ingenuity and fortitude to haul enormous logs to the mill behind straining oxen. It took courage and know-how to convert the logs to lumber and ship them through treacherous seas to market.

All these assets William Carson possessed. In 1863 he formed a partnership with an equally ingenious lumberman. John Dolbeer had invented a steam donkey engine that would make the straining oxen obsolete. Dolbeer & Carson operated four big mills, owned square miles of timber, commanded a fleet of lumber schooners.

It remained for William Carson to build his monument.

He decided on a stately home, one which would nail down his position as Eureka's first citizen. And in keeping with his status as lumber king, it would be built entirely of redwood, clear-grain and choice, the commodity that had made him rich. In 1884, Dolbeer & Carson mills were idle during a market slump, and the project would provide work for some of their best hands.

A hundred carpenters and artisans set to work, and the mansion began to rise. Three stories and a lordly tower, spacious porches and balconies, 18 rooms and wide hallways for the Carsons and their children, their retainers. To ornament the interior, Carson dispatched one of his ships to South America, brought back 97,000 feet of primavera, a light-colored hardwood. Arched recesses, soaring staircases, lofty panels were carved and embossed. Onyx fireplaces and stained glass added the sumptuous touch.

When the house was finished in 1886, journalists hailed it as indisputably the most magnificent in the West, and just possibly in the whole of America.

William Carson lived 26 years to enjoy his redwood mansion. When he died in 1912, his was the biggest funeral ever held in Eureka. His family stayed on in the home until 1950.

Now lovingly maintained by the prestigious Ingomar Club, the Carson Mansion is again the center of Humboldt County social life, and the delight of travelers to whom it re-creates an expansive era.

Interior archway, Carson Mansion.

Bret Harte: Embattled Editor at Arcata

Francis Bret Harte stepped ashore at Union Town, and eyed with disdain the long wharf over the northern Humboldt Bay mud flats. Young, elegant, and broke, the frontier poet had drifted to Humboldt Bay in 1857 via Brooklyn, Panama, Oakland, and the Sierra mines. Now he wondered how he would get to his sister's house without soiling his shoes. Maggie Harte had married the purser on a coasting schooner and come to settle in Union, at the bay's north terminus. Frank, or Bret, had failed to make a living in San Francisco, and he had come north to stay with Maggie.

Bret Harte's literary talent, which would produce "The Outcasts of Poker Flat" and "The Heathen Chinee," still lay unmined. But diligent prospectors of the day might have traced a vein of humor. Hearing that his hometown of Oakland had escaped damage in an earthquake, Harte quipped to San Franciscans: "There are some things even the earth cannot swallow."

Now he was on the beach. And the Union wharf was two miles long—that's what it took to connect the straggling village to tidewater. Pepperwood two-by-fours and an old white horse named Spanking Fury served as right-of-way and locomotive for the Union Plank Walk, Rail Track & Wharf Company, which did the connecting. Harte made the trip, joined Maggie, and found a job tutoring Captain Liscom's two sons at Mad River.

Harte lived three years at Union Town, and here he found his vocation. First he ran a school, clerked, and cut a figure for the local belles. Then in 1858, Colonel Stephen Whipple founded a weekly newspaper, *The Northern Californian,* and Harte hired out to him as a printer's devil. Quickly he found that ink fascinated him. He focused his attention, sharpened his wit, and became associate editor.

The colonel allowed Harte a free hand. In a feud with the Humboldt *Times* down in Eureka, Harte laid traps and snares which the *Times'* editors blundered into. Bret developed a clever biting style and seemed set for a country editor's career.

Then in February, 1860, Colonel Whipple went down to San Francisco, leaving young Harte in charge. On February 25, the current wave of Indian troubles culminated in a particularly unsavory massacre. A hundred women and children from a peaceful tribe had encamped on a bay island off Eureka. Ruffians fell on them at night and slew the helpless natives with knives and axes. Harte saw mutilated bodies carted through town like meat. He liked Indians, often talked with them. Now he acted.

Bret Harte in later life, living in England—a lionized author of the American West. At Uniontown (now Arcata), a hotelkeeper said of him: "He has the nose of genius—also his debts trouble him very little."

Above left: *Detail of a Danish cottage in Ferndale.* Above: *The town museum. Ferndale's main street has been repainted in soft pastel colors to recall Victorian era.* Left: *Redwood Gothic spires embellish a Ferndale church.*

That week's issue of *The Northern Californian* carried a searing editorial on the butchery and the butchers. Harte's prose rose to new heights in describing the atrocity, the wounds, the corpses. Whipple's readers took offense, for many of them limited good Indians to dead Indians. The publisher's purse was threatened, and he advised Harte to go.

Late in March, Bret Harte boarded the southbound *Columbia* for San Francisco. A fellow passenger was Undersheriff Henry McKay, absconding with $700 in county funds. (McKay sent back the key to the Eureka jail with the ship's pilot.)

On the 27th, Harte landed in San Francisco, ready to launch a new literary career. Before long he was editor of the West Coast's foremost magazine, and on his way to becoming a popular author.

When Alexander Brizard, Union's chief merchant, visited San Francisco, he was startled to see his old friend had put on airs. "Haw, haw, Brizard, haw *aw* you?" Harte greeted him, tugging at a full set of Dundrearies. Nor did he mention the old, cold days when Brizard had brought him firewood.

Yet memories of his years at Union were to haunt Bret Harte the rest of his life. They are echoed in compassionate yarns like "Three Vagabonds of Trinidad," written in England in 1900.

In this tale, an Indian boy, a dog, and a Chinese all perish under the heel of a "superior race."

Humboldt Bay was the cradle of lumber shipping as well as lumber.
Above, in 1892, the four-masted 970-ton barkentine Jane L. Stanford is
dressed for launching in Hans D. Bendixsen's yards at Fairhaven, south of
Eureka. She was the largest sailing vessel built in California up to that
time. After decades of service on the redwood coast, this graceful ship
ended her days as a fishing barge off San Pedro, run down and sunk by the
S.S. Humboldt in 1929. Smaller vessel on the ways is the three-masted bald-
headed schooner O. M. Kellogg, 393 tons. Bendixsen, a Danish shipwright,
came to Eureka in 1865 and built 113 wooden ships in 33 years' operation.
During World War I, demand for cargo ships was such that James Rolph,
later mayor of San Francisco and governor of California, bought the old yard
and built dozens of barkentines there. He also changed the name of
Fairhaven to Rolph. When the Armistice came, the yards closed.

Loading lumber at Eureka today.
Across the bay: the Georgia-Pacific
lumber mill at Samoa.

188

When the sea's running, Humboldt Bar is an exciting experience for pilots. This Greek freighter Stamatios Embiricos, *is* heading for the lumber wharves at Fairhaven. In the century after discovery of the Bay in 1850, 43 vessels were lost on the bar.

Dungeness crab, from Humboldt Bay, is a culinary attraction at Eureka.

The author displays an 18-pound king salmon off Humboldt Bar, a 20-minute trip by party boat from Eureka. Salmon season runs from early summer through late fall.

Flagship on the Bar

As Jonathan Winship or Hans Henry Buhne could testify, it took skill and a degree of luck to navigate across shallow, turbulent Humboldt Bar.

Many a stout bark never made it. The Bay entrance was a notorious maritime graveyard. A roster of headstones includes the S.S. *Brooklyn* (19 lives lost); schooner *Corinthian* (2 lives); schooner *Mexican* (4 lives); steamer *Chilkat* (9 lives); schooner *Fidelity* (6 lives); bark *Hartford* (2 lives); brig *Willimentic* (8 lives); schooner *Laura Pike* (7 lives). And there were more.

Many vessels foundered outside the Bay, on treacherous North or South Spit. Shifting sand, riptides, and offshore currents made the portals of Humboldt a fearsome place.

Therefore it is puzzling to contemplate with what degree of disrespect the United States Navy treated these sandy shoals in 1916–1917. It was to cost the brass hats their finest ship, the U.S.S. *Milwaukee*, a 9,700-ton heavy cruiser, flagship of the Pacific Fleet.

As Richard H. Dillon tells the tale in *The Siren Sub of Samoa Beach*, the bait was an iron-hulled lady, the submarine *H-3*. Entering the Bay on December 14, 1916, *H-3* grounded on the North, or Samoa Spit, five miles from the harbor mouth. Her crew was rescued by Coast Guard lifeboats, but *H-3* stuck fast.

For a week, Navy tugs and monitors hauled at *H-3*, trying to pry her loose. Finally Rear Admiral William B. Caperton, Commander in Chief of the Pacific Fleet, brought up *Milwaukee*. Her 21,000 horsepower, her 24 tons of cable would free the sub. Belching smoke, the cruiser's pull began. Still *H-3* refused to budge, and now something unforseen occurred.

The strain parted a hawser with which one monitor was holding *Milwaukee*'s head to sea. In minutes her own cables dragged the proud cruiser onto the beach beside the submarine. Broadside, canted at a 20-degree list, the flagship and her complement of 449 were helpless in the breakers.

With every surge, *Milwaukee* inched a little higher on the sand. She was at last seated so firmly that the red-faced Navy never tried to get her off.

Eventually she was scrapped—the government built a trestle out to the beached cruiser and took out her guns, engines, and equipment. In years to come, and as the hulk slowly disintegrated, it was accepted as part of the scenery. Fishermen used it as a platform from which to catch cod, bass, and crabs. Daring youths used it as a jungle gym, climbing masts, running 'tween decks where hatches banged mournfully. Finally *Milwaukee*'s remains were blasted loose during the Second World War for scrap metal.

Anxious passengers line the rails as the steamer Corona *broaches on Humboldt Bar, March 1, 1907. Coast Guardsmen rescued all but one of her complement, but the 1,492-ton steel craft soon broke up under heavy pounding.*

The cause of it all: United States Submarine H-3, sometimes called Garfish, *fast in the sand on Samoa spit, January, 1917. Eurekans inspect the stranded warship before the heavy cruiser* Milwaukee *made fast with heavy cable in her ill-fated towing attempt.*

Coast Guardsmen row Milwaukee *crewmen ashore on January 13, 1917, after 9,700-ton flagship beached in 12 feet of water while attempting to tow off the submarine. Sailors wait their turn at the rails.*

The Navy admits defeat. U.S.S. Milwaukee *under salvage (right), a trestle touching her sides, begins her long agony of breakup on the Humboldt sands.*

And what of the "siren sub" that lured the mighty cruiser to destruction?

Jim Fraser, local contractor and ex-logger, offered to salvage her for $18,000. Though the Navy privately considered Fraser mentally unbalanced, he got the job. Instead of trying to haul *H-3* out to sea, the old woodsman headed in the opposite direction. He jacked the submarine up like a redwood log, and with steam engines and rollers, towed the tin Lorelei a full mile across the sandbar into Humboldt Bay.

H-3 was taken down to Mare Island and put to work as a training ship. Her skipper, and the towing officer of the *Milwaukee,* were formally charged with neglect, but wartime intervened and they were never court-martialed.

At such cost did the U. S. Navy learn respect for the Humboldt Bar.

Fishing is big business when the salmon run at Eureka. Barely 20 minutes from the docks at Fields Landing, 40-pounders lurk in summer and autumn.

Across the sparkling waters of Humboldt Bay, the $20 million atomic power plant of Pacific Gas & Electric Company supplies "juice" for Eureka, and the northern Redwood Empire. Completed in 1962, the plant was the utility's second venture into commercial power from nuclear sources. Its initial loading was 17.3 tons of uranium fuel. The company's announced aim is to produce kilowatts— 60,000 of them—in its boiling-water reactor as cheaply as is normally done by fossil fuels.

*Gulls add motion to
a quiet fishing dock in Eureka.*

*And there is the rain . . .
in this case at Samoa,
across the bay from Eureka.*

The north country is a hard country . . . if it isn't fire, it's flood. Near Weott, wet winter of 1960.

. . . or depression. Relic near Fieldbrook, Humboldt County.

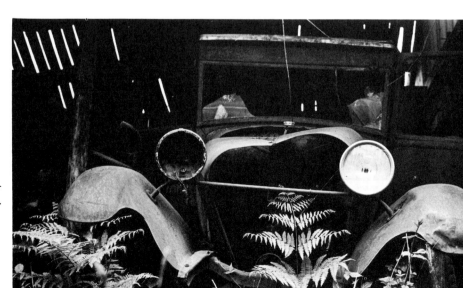

But the compensations are great; even the fog has its admirers. Beach near Trinidad.

And nature comes closer than almost anywhere. Roosevelt elk at Prairie Creek.

Headland and drift logs, Dry Lagoon
—on the northern Humboldt Coast.

Surf against weathered log, Dry Lagoon.

There are quiet byways to explore in Humboldt County, like this one above the Trinity River between Willow Creek and the Indian Reservation at Hoopa. Up this narrow canyon Jedediah Smith and his fur traders struggled in 1828. A famous salmon and steelhead stream, the Trinity runs deceivingly shallow in summer.

Ingenuity delights the eye, as at Fallbrook, almost deserted lumber town, where a householder found this redwood stump a natural roost for his redwood water tank.

198

From the vanished age . . . one of two remaining covered bridges over Elk Creek, southeast of Eureka.

Sun, woods, and water far from the traveled highroad. . . . Red Cap Creek, southwest of Orleans.

The North Coast: The Law Beyond the Klamath

"Money? We don't use money north of the Klamath—only clamshells and woodpecker scalps."

Thus colorful Judge John L. Childs of Crescent City represented California's northwestern corner to a legislative committee in Sacramento.

Truth was, the region *did* fall back on Indian barter during the 1933 bank holiday. Clamshells marked "Good For 10¢" were used for small change. There is no confirmation that the ancient Yurok medium, topknots of the redheaded woodpecker, brought $5.

Independence and a certain brusque view of formal legality persists in Del Norte County. A recent district attorney told a private client: "I advised the county to order you to do such-and-such, but *I* tell you to ignore it." It is a matter of pride that the town of Klamath never knew a depression during Prohibition. Spirits were in good supply and boys were trained to stalk prowling agents from "down below."

Klamath and its neighbors showed their mettle during the terrible floods of 1964. John Menary ignored $20,000 worth of liquor in his store when the waters began to rise. Instead he loaded his neighbor's sheep into the rescue truck. Jack Morris, motel owner, threw open his rooms to Klamath refugees, never did count what it cost him to feed the homeless ones for three weeks. Babe Crivelli and Tony Ramos, flooded out in 1955, lost everything all over again in 1964. Both were back in business with restaurants and stores by the following April. Crivelli hadn't finished paying off the federal loan he took after the '55 disaster.

California's northwest coast still holds to the frontier ethic. Pledged words and character count highest. Remote, and to some forbidding, the region remains a sportsman's paradise. Del Norte County's total population is only about 14,000, and 72 percent of its land is government-owned. This, combined with the precariousness of its lumber-based economy, makes for pride—and hard scrabble.

Gold opened the County of the North. News of the gold strike on the Trinity siphoned prospectors north from San Francisco.

Judge John L. Childs, a political power in Del Norte County for 60 years. Photo was made by A. W. Ericson when the colorful jurist was a young man.

Horace Gasquet: engineer, innkeeper— and duelist.

In 1850 an even more glittering strike was reported, at Gold Bluffs, just south of the Klamath. The precious metal was right there in the black sand! An official of the quickly organized Pacific Mining Company informed the *Alta California* early in 1851: if the beach is only a tenth as rich as it looks, "it would be enough to yield each shareholder $43 million."

This heady stuff sent prospecting fleets skimming north to the Bluffs. Alas, though hundreds labored to separate the golden particles from the sand, there was too much sand and too few particles.

The disappointed prospectors turned inland. Almost at once they hit it rich on the Illinois River, across the Oregon border. Sailors Diggings, Althouse, Jacksonville, and other camps yielded fortunes in dust and nuggets. The supply port of Crescent City was hewn from beach and forest.

Hubert Howe Bancroft, later California's foremost historian, came there to establish a bookstore in 1853. He noted "there is more crescent than city": a few split-board shanties trembled "between the sullen roar of the ocean" and the dense forest. On Sundays there were amusements: "Horse racing, foot racing and cock-fighting on the beach." Bancroft returned to San Francisco after two years with a stake of $8,000. Evidently Crescent City was literate.

The first lumber mill was established in 1853. Planks were not exported until 1869 when a larger plant was built at Lake Earl by A. M. Simpson and Jacob Wenger. From a quarter section, 160 acres, the partners took 35 million board feet of redwood. Some acres yielded a million feet apiece.

Caleb Hobbs and J. E. Wall also joined to establish a lumber, mercantile, and shipping business which would dominate Crescent City's economic life for 73 years. Miles of timber, a fleet of schooners, railroads, and the Coast's largest box factory carried the Hobbs-Wall brand.

The principal occupation in Crescent City's hatching days was freighting supplies over the mountains to the mines. Buckskin-clad packers and traders thronged the streets. Mule trains left daily for Sailors Diggings, Happy Camp, and Jacksonville. Horace Gasquet, a French engineer who had fled his homeland as the aftermath of a duel, established a hotel 15 miles inland and built a notable 23-mile toll road over the precipices to Oregon. Gasquet charged pedestrians 25 cents to use his road. Sheep and hogs were 6 cents apiece, horsemen a dollar, and a two-horse wagon $3. Today the road is still in use, free, by man or hog.

Despite its promise, Del Norte remained isolated behind the rivers and mountains. Attempts to build railroad links fizzled. A Los Angeles syndicate tried to promote a harbor. Finally in the 1920's all factions united in an effort to get a highway system. The Klamath was bridged in 1926. Soon roads led across the mountains to Grants Pass and up the Oregon coast, past Smith River.

Though the barriers were breached, Del Norte remained self-sufficient. The county reserves its admiration for men like Babe Crivelli and Tony Ramos, and for those who stubbornly defied defeat when a "tsunami" wave from the Alaska earthquake engulfed downtown Crescent City on Good Friday, 1964, taking 11 lives and smashing most of the business district.

"Comeback Town U.S.A.," Crescent City dubbed itself. The town's redevelopment plans include a shopping mall and a beachfront recreation center.

Crescent City in the 1850's,
"more crescent than city."
From an old engraving.

The Fatal *Brother Jonathan*

Of all California's maritime disasters, the deadliest was the wreck of the *Brother Jonathan*.

The 1,500-ton side-wheel steamer foundered on St. George Reef, off Crescent City, on the blustery afternoon of July 30, 1865. Two hundred men, women, and children were drowned, including an Army general and the Governor of Washington.

The story is a tragedy of greed, cowardice, and mischance.

Once a Vanderbilt-owned ship in the Nicaragua run, the *Brother Jonathan* by 1865 was leaky, wheezy, and obsolete. When she sailed from San Francisco on July 27, she was gravely overloaded. Her destination was the Pacific Northwest, a region hungry for supplies. Captain Samuel deWolf protested when the owners filled the *Brother Jonathan* until she rode four feet deeper than what he considered safe. He was told to keep quiet or look for another job.

With 174 passengers and a crew of 50, the *Brother Jonathan* labored north against heavy seas, making Crescent City harbor on July 29. Joseph Lord, a Wells Fargo messenger, who was carrying $140,000 in gold for the express company, was especially pleased at the stopover. His wife and daughter were in Crescent City. But important passengers like Brigadier General George Wright, en route to command the Department of the Columbia, and Dr. Anson Henry, personal friend of President Lincoln and newly appointed Governor of Washington Territory, were anxious for the voyage to resume.

After some debate about venturing into the gale, Captain deWolf cast off lines and steamed out, heading northwest. By noon, wind and waves had increased and his ship was at a standstill. So overladen was the *Brother Jonathan* that her ancient boilers refused to drive her. Captain deWolf ordered her turned back to port. But the laboring vessel had meanwhile drifted close to the seething rocks of St. George Reef, eight miles offshore. Just before two o'clock, the *Brother Jonathan* struck heavily, springing her planks and bringing the foremast down through the deck. As her keel broke and her bottom tore away, the captain ordered "abandon ship."

The first lifeboat was lowered. It capsized and its passengers drowned before the eyes of those on deck. A second boat suffered the same fate. The third boat, smallest on the ship, then put out under command of Third Officer James Patterson. It contained five women, three children, and ten crewmen who had jumped aboard before more women and youngsters could take their places.

"Tell them," Captain deWolf shouted at Patterson through the gale, "tell them if they had not overloaded us, we would have got through all right." There were no more lifeboats.

Patterson's cockleboat, shipping water from the heavy sea, threaded through a ghastly flotsam: drowned and floating bodies, "women . . . their hair loose and outspread." The passengers could see General Wright standing on deck, his military cloak wrapped around his wife. She had refused to leave without him.

For two hours Patterson's crew rowed for shore. At first they could see the doomed ship when they topped a wave. They lost sight of her when the boat descended into the trough. Finally after one ascent the watchers looked in vain for the *Brother Jonathan*. She had disappeared.

On the beach, rescue parties put out, guided by the exhausted Patterson. They found nothing but wreckage and bodies.

A few days later the body of James Nesbit, editor of the San Francisco *Bulletin*, washed up on the beach. Buttoned inside his shirt, wrapped in oilskin, was Nesbit's will—and a letter. He had written it while standing on deck, awaiting the *Brother Jonathan*'s death throes.

"You spoke of me sailing on Friday—hangman's day—and the unlucky Jonathan," the editor wrote. "Well here I am with death before me. My love to you all."

Above right: *St. George Light, six miles west of Crescent City, is resupplied in a storm. Completed at immense effort in 1891, it cost $702,000 and was one of world's costliest lighthouses. Every other Tuesday, the Coast Guard relieves two of St. George's crew of seven. It was nearby on the offshore reef in 1865 that California's ghastliest shipwreck took place.* Below right: *State historical marker at old cemetery on Crescent City bluffs. Here a few of the* Brother Jonathan *victims are buried. Some were dance-hall girls en route to new goldfields.*

The fatal Brother Jonathan.

Survey crew near Crescent City in the 1890's. They were laying out line for Santa Fe Railroad, never built. Transportation was a plaguing concern in Del Norte County for almost a century.

County roads in Del Norte sometimes had to have a base of split redwood planks, especially where soil was shifting. This buggy route antedated U.S. Highway 101 south of Crescent City.

Above: *North of Orick in the 1920's, the Redwood Highway (U.S. 101) was built by Ford dump trucks with one-yard beds, on a long fill. Three shifts worked 24 hours a day. Below: Building the Redwood Highway north of Orick in remote Humboldt County, Englehart Paving & Construction Co. noted that "graders, tractors and 'fresnoes' were used to keep the roadbed in shape, without results. Fordson Iron Mules later were resorted to," and that worked.*

205

This high-wheeled International Harvester conveyance served as the Crescent City–Grants Pass stage in 1914. It was a trip to try men's souls.

Battery Point Lighthouse at Crescent City, built in 1856 and one of the oldest in the West, is now a museum, visited at low tide.

Logged land near Lake Earl, north of Crescent City. According to report, politicians wanted to settle displaced Indians on this devastated and worthless tract. They were foiled by Judge John L. Childs, who insisted on better homesites at the mouth of the Smith River, some of which the tribes occupy today.

One of California's most spectacular beaches, near Crescent City. Too cold for swimming, but great for strolling and driftwood picking.

*Fog shrouds their crowns and ferns garland
their feet . . . giant redwoods crowd old
stagecoach road east of Crescent City in
Jedediah Smith State Park.*

*Easter lily fields carpet the Smith
River area in July. Del Norte
County produces both massive and
delicate flora.*

Sports pressure builds up to this extremity when king
salmon run each fall at the Klamath. Anglers cast
elbow-to-elbow in the lagoon inside the river mouth.
Their rivals—policed by Coast Guardsmen—fish from
skiffs. Lures cast into a boat by beach fishermen
seldom find their way back to the owner, and
fistfights sometimes enliven the fishing.

She has a king salmon hooked, and
now the trick is to land him while
avoiding neighbors' lines.

The salmon fleet awaits a run on the Klamath. Some call it "Suicide Row."

He has a 12-pound silverside salmon, blooded from a landing gaff. At the mouth of the Smith River.

*Sword ferns festoon the butt end
of a fallen redwood in the Del Norte woods.*

Rain-washed boulders beside the Smith River.

Howard C. Tibbits made this photograph of virgin
redwoods behind a rail fence at Camp Grant, on the
Eel River near Dyerville, in the 1890's. Titled "The
Mystery of the Forest," it has helped Save-the-
Redwoods League raise more than $10 million from
ardent conservationists since 1918. The grove has
been logged off, which adds poignancy to the league's
appeal for funds.

From tree to "cold deck." Douglas fir logs await the sawyer's pleasure near Arcata. Of 108 billion board feet of timber now standing in the redwood region, an estimated 31 billion is redwood, 64 billion Douglas fir, the balance other softwoods, such as pine. The term "cold deck" stems from mills' practice of stacking logs for use during the winter, when loggers can't get into forests.

Redwoods Feed the Fires
of Controversy: What Price Tall Trees?

Like floods and fires, conflict seems inevitable in the redwood country. In its larger-than-life setting, trappers battled the wilderness, settlers fought Indians, engineers assaulted mountains, sailors braved the sea.

Strong men with strong opinions tamed the land of giants. Now in the old arena their descendants face a new kind of strife, a battle whose causes are only dimly perceived, but whose effects are feared like a Yurok raid. This conflict has many names: vandals against trees, poetry versus economics, sentiment against fact.

William Carson and his roughhewn sidekicks saw life uncomplicated by social conscience. Their job was to cut and saw redwoods, ship them to market. In gold-rush San Francisco, Yankee artisans were building homes and stores of the native wood, improving on the Mexicans' mud and stone. Demand for handsome, rot-resistant redwood was heavy, so by 1860 three hundred sawmills screeched between Monterey and Oregon. Soon thereafter railroads and portable engines made possible logging on the grand scale. In some places the redwoods seen by Father Font and Mr. Carson vanished.

To many observers this heralded the extinction of a noble breed. In 1859, Bayard Taylor, the Eastern author, described "the Pikes," who were Missouri forerunners of the Okies, taking positive glee in leveling redwoods. Robert Louis Stevenson commented sadly on the fate of Silverado's sequoias and its Indians: by 1880 ". . . all had already perished . . . the two noblest indigenous living things, alike condemned." In 1884 a San Francisco newspaper reported loggers had usurped the redwood crown of Contra Costa's hills; and John Muir lamented that not even the Lord could save sequoias from the saws, it was up to Uncle Sam.

Such shrill alarms had their political echo. The literary bellwethers aroused nationwide concern over the redwoods, and intellectuals and men of goodwill joined to apply legislative pressure. In 1885 California established a Board of Forestry to curb wasteful logging. The Sempervirens Club demanded protection for groves near Santa Cruz, whereupon in 1901 the state established its first park at Big Basin, to preserve those Coast redwoods. Gifford Pinchot of Pennsylvania, father of the national forests, began conservation studies in the U.S. Department of Agriculture in 1899; and at his urging, President Theodore

Bill Stevens fells a mature redwood in Georgia-Pacific's woods near Big Lagoon, Humboldt County. With a gasoline-driven chain saw, the job is accomplished in a few minutes, but it still takes skill.

216

Spare that tree! President Herbert Hoover joins hands with members of a redwoods expedition in the 1920's to illustrate the girth of the famous Stout Tree, in Del Norte County. This almost-perfect redwood is 20 feet in diameter at eye level, 340 feet tall. It is preserved in the National Tribute Grove.

Roosevelt set aside the Monterey Forest Reserve in 1906. He also accepted Muir Woods National Monument in 1908 from generous William Kent.

The fight to save *S. sempervirens* from the sawmills had begun, but a fresh peril appeared. The success of the plan to build a Redwood Highway into Humboldt County implied both arrival of population and removal of obstacle trees. This threat spurred three eminent conservationists in 1918 to form the Save-the-Redwoods League. One of the trio, Madison Grant, secretary of the New York Zoological Society, wrote this ironic note in the society's bulletin for September, 1919:

"Development of the vineyards is the most immediate and threatening danger to the redwoods of California. These superb trees are sacrificed to supply the stakes to carry vines, because of the particularly indestructible character of their wood, which will stand in the ground almost indefinitely without rotting."

Circulating warnings, reinforced with heart-moving photos of the threatened groves, the league since 1918 has raised more than $12 million from philanthropists and nature-lovers. It has used these funds to purchase redwood groves. Since 1928 the State of California has "matched" league funds, and by 1966 a total of 109,367 acres lay inviolate in redwood region parks, largely as a result of league efforts.

But some redwood lovers are by no means satisfied. Most vocal on this score is the 34,000-member Sierra Club, founded in 1892 by John Muir himself, which wants to protect still more forests. Backed by a million-dollar annual budget, Sierra Club spokesmen subscribe to Thoreau's credo: "In wildness is the preservation of the world." This goes a long step beyond conservation, or at least beyond those who believe nature and enlightened industry can live together in the woods. In 1963 the Sierra Club focused its influence on realizing a long-cherished project—a National Redwoods Park.

The concept was not new. In 1946, Congresswoman Helen Gahagan Douglas had submitted bills creating the Franklin D. Roosevelt Memorial Forest, 2½ million acres, with about 180,000 in redwoods. Mrs. Douglas' bills failed, but the Sierra Club and its allies determined to try again, and only for redwoods. Secretary of the Interior Stewart Udall, who had helped establish the Point Reyes National Seashore, was enthusiastic. So was the National Geographic Society and its president, Melville Bell Grosvenor. The society's first step was to allot $64,000 to the National Park Service, specifically "to study the Coast redwood and its environment."

A proposal to improve the Redwood Highway, U.S. 101, at Prairie Creek State Park in upper Humboldt County, helped bring the issue of erecting a National Redwoods Park to a head. California's Division of Highways was studying routes for a new four-lane strip to replace a two-lane road, vintage of the

217

1920's, which twists for eight miles through stately groves. Rather than widen the present road and destroy several hundred huge trees, state engineers suggested alternate routes. The most likely of these would have run along the adjacent beach, at the foot of Gold Bluffs. Any feasible route, however, would remove redwoods, some on state park property, most on private lands. The Sierra Club joined by park staffers, vowed to fight the loss of any trees—and the "wild" beach, too. Governor Edmund G. Brown involved himself, declaring that he would veto removal of even one redwood in any state park, though he later modified this statement.

Spearhead of the Sierra Club's battle plan was a sumptuous photographic book, *The Last Redwoods*, by François Leydet, published by the club late in 1963. The volume's title sums up its theme. "Red-woods—going, going . . ." one caption reads. The text warns: "With every suburbanite who repanels his living room with redwood the end of the great trees draws nearer." And Leydet declares: "Within a few years, the remnants of the virgin forest will be gone." Documenting his words with photos of stumps and jackstraw log piles, the author indicts the lumber companies, the highway department, and the forestry profession for crimes against the big trees.

The Last Redwoods was widely reviewed. It provoked numerous sympathetic magazine articles with comment critical of lumbermen and freeway engineers. "Good-bye to the Redwoods?" and "Redwoods—Doomed" were typical titles. Leydet had concluded that only a national park could save the surviving titans. The chorus that followed echoed this point of view.

Meanwhile the National Geographic Society, conducting its study in conjunction with the Park Service, measured some extraordinary redwoods southeast of Orick, a few miles from Prairie Creek. In a story in the *National Geographic Magazine,* one tree was described as the Mount Everest of All Living Things, a sequoia 367.8 feet tall; two neighboring spires were almost as lofty. The story stirred fresh interest in redwood preservation.

Would these forest mammoths feel the ax? Their owner said no. But the very question aroused new uneasiness. A few months later, in the fall of 1964, the National Park Service issued its interim report: thousands of additional redwood acres should be placed under Federal protection, in a national park. Three plans were advanced, embracing forests in north coastal Humboldt County and neighboring Del Norte. All centered on a trio of existing state parks: Prairie Creek (10,289 acres) in northern Humboldt; Del Norte Coast Redwoods (5,932 acres); and Jedediah Smith (9,539 acres) in Del Norte County. Additional watershed, beach, and private forest would be added to these three to round out a national park somewhere between 32,000 and 62,000 acres. Through the park no freeway would be permitted to go, and no trees could be cut.

In the north counties, this bureaucratic largesse was greeted like a skunk in church. A third of Humboldt and three-quarters of Del Norte were already government-owned—exempt from the taxes of county, city, school, and fire district. Subtracting more taxable land would invite ruin, local officials protested. Worse, much of the national park acreage would come out of the "industrial" forests of lumber firms, which had counted on this unfailing woodland bank for future withdrawals. Based on this same assumption, two huge pulp mills had just begun $90 million worth of construction near Eureka. Preemption of their raw materials by the national park would jeopardize the largest investment ever made in the redwood country.

Caught between the twin grindstones of economic survival and aroused public opinion, the people who live in the shade of the redwoods are feeling the squeeze. In Del Norte, Humboldt, and Mendocino counties 17,000 men and women work directly for the forest industries; another 34,000 service their needs. "One out of every four persons living in these counties," an industry spokesman maintained, "owes his paycheck to trees."

At issue is a present annual payroll of $104 million, capital investment of three times that much. Shipping, schools, stores, life itself in the northern counties, all depend on timber. Thus creation of a national park seemed to many to foreshadow a new Appalachia.

On February 23, 1966, an Administration-supported bill was introduced in Congress, proposing establishment of a 44,800-acre Redwood National Park, with 43,400 acres in Del Norte County (embracing Jedediah Smith State Park and Del Norte Redwoods State Park, with woodlands connecting them) and 1,400 acres in Humboldt County, surrounding the "tallest trees" on Redwood Creek. Purchase cost was estimated at $56,850,000 and the Federal Government also proposed $342,000 a year for five years in economic aid to the counties, to offset loss of taxes.

Under the plan, the Federal Government would spend another $4 million to buy property adjoining Prairie Creek and Humboldt Redwood State Parks and donate this to the State of California, in ex-

World's tallest living things, Coast Redwoods exceeding 367 feet in height, were discovered recently beside Redwood Creek in northern Humboldt County.

Not only humans are embattled in the redwood country.
These bull elk (right) at Prairie Creek State Park
decided to settle their differences in the traffic lanes on
Highway 101.

change for the two state parks to be taken. It would also transfer to the state Muir Woods National Monument and 31,000 acres of Bureau of Land Management property in the King Range.

Lumber industry spokesmen thought this plan the lesser of several evils, but some said they would continue to oppose any national park as "only the beginning of an ultimate takeover of all redwood lands." Save-the-Redwoods League officials hailed any national park move as a good one, but Sierra Club spokesmen said the Administration plan was "too small, and in the wrong place."

It was apparent the controversy was nowhere near resolution.

Late in 1966, hearings were to begin in Washington and in California on the National Redwood Park. John Muir's Uncle Sam still held the Key, or so it seemed to many, but the doors were yet to be opened.

219

Gold Bluffs beach.
Saved forever from the
concrete juggernaut?

Highway 101 at Prairie
Creek State Park.
Nobody—not even the state engineers
—wanted to widen it.

Industry's Responsibility; Population's Threat

There is room for everything, including argument, in the redwood country. Especially, nowadays, argument over the regional namesake.

Poets argue that each tree felled represents the desecration of a "noble place of worship." To foresters, this is so much humbug.

In *The Last Redwoods*, François Leydet imputes a kind of immortality to the trees, saying, ". . . there is no biological reason why one should ever die."

Foresters chop this thesis into shingle bolts. Emanuel Fritz, professor emeritus of forestry at the University of California, who has made a lifelong study of redwoods, says in a review of Leydet's book:

"The public has been given the impression that all redwood trees are immense in size and hoary with age. The fact is, a tree [Coast Redwood] 1800 years old or older is a great rarity." Fritz put the death of redwoods into another perspective:

"Fires and heavy winds killed far more of them over the centuries than loggers. It would make more sense to concentrate on preventing fires and wind damage than to halt commercial cutting."

Preservationists think otherwise. Many people are involved emotionally with these great trees, and they see modern man as the chief menace. In 1964, the National Park Service reported: "We find striking inherent conflict between [the redwood's] value for harvest and for preservation. Here is a tree with singular market demand as lumber, growing in what is perhaps the most productive forest land in the world. Here, too, this same tree is one of the most unique and outstanding in the world in justifying preservation."

A hundred authors bear witness. Redwoods are a dramatic link with the past. "Ambassadors from another time," John Steinbeck calls them. Aeons ago, they covered most of the northern world. Then glaciers and changing climate pushed them to the verge of extinction, exempting only a thin strip on the northern California coast, plus some bulkier cousins in the high Sierra.

Preservation fighters make an earnest case for their concern. From nearly two million red-wooded acres before the loggers came, the untouched or "old growth" stand is down to about 365,000. The Sierra Club and the National Park Service point to this shrinkage as—in the words of a club film script—"a heritage of devastation." The Park Service holds that California's 110,000 acres of state redwood parks are only "nominally preserved" from the threat of highways and floods caused by logged-off tracts upstream. The clear implication is that the Federal Government can do it better.

If 1.6 million acres of redwood have indeed been "lost" since the 1850's, it would most surely seem that the big trees are doomed. But, total redwood acreage today is 1,687,000, only a little less than in Indian times, according to a "white paper" issued in 1964 by American Forest Products Industries, in San Francisco. Of this total, 365,000 acres indeed are classed as "old growth," or virgin forest; of this ancient acreage, 118,000 at that time was in public preserves and 247,000 in private ownership.

Determining the age and growth rate of "new" redwoods on Union Lumber Company land. Professor Emanuel Fritz (left) counsels Forester Robert Grundeman, who examines specimen taken from within tree by auger-like increment borer, still sunk deep in the wood. Tree is "shoot" pushed up by original redwood, cut perhaps 70 years ago. It remains undamaged by this test.

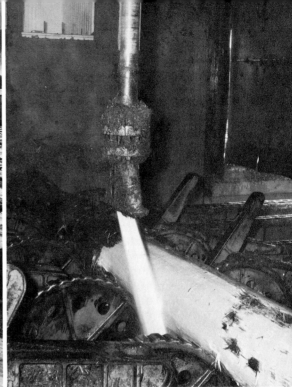

Left: *Log pond at The Pacific Lumber Company mill, Scotia. Redwood lengths are dumped here from trucks before being moved to the sawmill for debarking. Scotia installation is largest redwood mill in the world, welcomes visitors, who are permitted to take a self-guided tour. Hills at left were logged 70 years ago, now display healthy second-growth trees. Right: Fourteen hundred pounds of water pressure peels the bark from this log in Union Lumber Company mill, Fort Bragg. The hydraulic barker can strip a 12-foot log in three minutes.*

What remains, says the AFPI report, is 1,322,000 acres of young growth, much of it logged between the time Fort Ross was built in 1812, and the beginning of World War I. "Young growth" for a redwood forest does not imply saplings: many of these trees are six to eight feet thick. Of this "young forest," 109,000 acres are in public domain, making an aggregate of 227,000 acres preserved—young and old. The balance of the young timber, 1,213,000 acres, is privately owned. Being young and possessed of redwood's unique vigor, it increased in board-foot volume 56 percent between 1952 and 1964. This measured volume is expected to double by the year 2000.

Old-growth woods continue to be cut, but it is from this young reserve that most redwood of the future will be drawn. Forester John G. Miles forecasts that by 1995 the 247,000 acres of privately owned virgin forest will be gone—logged *or taken for parks.* Henceforth the big mills will harvest increasingly from a never-failing bank account, woods 50 and 60 years old. In them scattered old-growth seed trees will be left, so that in the "managed" forest a percentage of giants always will be present.

Despite such expressed concepts of responsible forestry, preservationists continue to sound the alarm. Redwood cutting, they point out, has almost doubled. From an annual average of 500 million board feet before World War II, it now runs around 850 million. (A board foot is 12 inches square, one inch thick.) According to a U.S. Forest Service projection made in 1960, practically all the virgin redwood in private hands would be gone by 1980.

Writers since before the days of John Muir have predicted the total extinction of the redwoods. But lumbermen meanwhile have discovered the value of conservation practices, and the big operators farm and harvest trees scientifically, just to stay in business. In this they are aided materially by the redwood's inherent vitality. Given adequate light, air, and water, *Sequoia sempervirens* sprouts anew from stumps

223

and seedlings at the rate of a foot or two each year. Thus the descendants of trees that William Carson logged are ripe for the market now, and a continuous supply of redwood for home and industry seems assured.

This does nothing to console the preservationists. Their concern is not for market supply, but for aesthetics, for morality. The extremists among them demand that all cutting of redwoods cease, even if it puts the mills out of business and their employees out of jobs. On the surface, the rift often seems a matter of degree: how much redwood is enough for the mills, for the parks? Is logging under present conditions damaging the eternal supply? Or is nature gaining on the chain saw?

Actually the conflict runs deeper, between the sheer headlands of commerce and idealism. The lumbermen claim their replenishment system works. The preservationists reply "so what?"; even if it does, profiting from the death of redwoods is wicked, and great moral harm comes from commercial destruction of irreplaceable trees.

Are "virgin" or old-growth redwoods really irreplaceable? Emanuel Fritz says: "The word 'virgin' applied to redwoods is a misnomer. Those giants we see are actually the thousandth crop, in the millionth year, or more." According to fossil testimony, redwoods existed in much their present form 40 million years ago. They rise again, Phoenix-like, after fires and storms. Now that commerce has gained wisdom about them, man's inroads can be repaired by time and by men.

Fritz considers that the spectacular groves, those travelers come to see, are comparatively rare. They flourish only on river benches—flat surfaces close to active streams, where roots run close to water and floods deposit nourishing silt. In such natural hothouses, coastal sequoias attain their ultimate majesty in a climax forest, their deep shade and preempting root systems excluding lesser vegetation.

Only a fraction of the groves are of this "climax forest" quality, and almost all of these magnificent river flats already lie protected in state parks. Professor Fritz thinks that, regarding marginal or hillside groves which are as yet unprotected, "no tourist would go from the Atlantic to the Pacific to see the general run of redwood forest." One and a half million large, original-growth trees are in public ownership today, a degree of preservation for this species "far beyond what had been accomplished with any other timber resource in the nation," according to another forester, John T. Keane. Still another 8,000 acres of superlative stand are being held inviolate by the large lumber firms, to be added to the state parks as purchase funds become available.

Examining the moral side does little to unravel the knot. Is it better morality to cut a young tree than an old one? More admirable to fell a big cypress, oak, or Douglas fir than a middle-sized redwood? Why not, one exasperated Eurekan suggests, preserve the tall cornstalks of Iowa? Morality or mystique, the fact remains that influential citizens in Los Angeles, New York, and elsewhere are deeply committed to save all redwoods, and they work hard to protect them from sawmills and freeways.

For this current upsurge of emotion, the redwood industry must accept a full share of blame. Until recently, the lumbermen were split internally over cutting practices, and the industry was notorious for its relations with the public, scornfully underestimating the preservationists' ardor. In 1949 and again in 1960 industry consultants including Professor Fritz in vain urged a ban on logging near highways, and on clear-cutting—denuding the land.

One celebrated example of how this advice was ignored took place near Orick, beside the Redwood Highway itself, in full view of several million motorists. Entire hillsides were clear-logged and left covered with unsightly slash and stumps, not far from a state park whose pristine trees furnished ironic contrast. Leydet's book calls this particular cut "apocalyptic devastation," and it is cited in every preservation report.

Professor Fritz says the Orick owner tried selective cutting for a decade, only to find it impractical on the hilly site because of soil and wind: the trees that had been selected to remain blew down with disastrous results. So the company clear-logged, then tried to appease the passing public by erecting roadside conservation exhibits, explaining its reforestation program. But the scar will remain until time erases it. In the eyes of nature-lovers, the forest was raped.

On the plus side, the redwood industry's tree-farm program has shown quiet results. Almost 650,000 acres now stand in renewal forests. But tree farming is still permissive, not mandatory, and conservationists want stronger laws. They quote erosion statistics on selectively logged "farms." They cite failure of the state to prosecute companies that violate its Forest Practices Act. The classic example, says the Sierra Club, is the downstream flood devastation on Bull Creek, caused, they believe, by improper logging in the fir forests higher up.

It still takes plenty of man to handle the big logs. Truckdriver and loader tighten
binders on several tons of redwood log near Arcata.

Emanuel Fritz, nearing 80, saw the last of the great old days in the woods when he came west in 1919. He has served as consultant in forestry to the Department of the Interior, the California legislature, and the Save-the-Redwoods League. He is famous for his nature walks at the annual Bohemian Grove encampment.

The old skills survive at the annual Loggers & Lumbermen's Jubilee in Arcata. This high-climbing jack has swarmed up a lofty pole wearing belt and spikes, and has sawed loose a section to win the topping competition.

On a hillside in Humboldt County, distant
from public highways, and from tourists'
view, The Pacific Lumber Company practices
selective cutting and natural reseeding.
After foresters study and mark trees to be
cut, loggers remove them, leaving stumps
(foreground). Freed from forest competition,
the remaining trees (called "residuals")
increase their growth rate many times. They
also shed cones which provide seeds for
new small trees. The old stumps sprout new
trees, which in three or four human
generations, almost equal their original
parents in size.

Preservationism demands a halt to all redwood logging until "selective" cutting can be scientifically evaluated. "Maybe they want to kill the patient before he goes broke," Professor Fritz remarks.

The Sierra Club and its allies argue that "selective cutting" should not be accepted as conservation where "unique treasures" like virgin forests are concerned. Here the basic conflict is exposed: "stop cutting" versus "continue in business." To compromise such positions seems impossible.

The fall of 1964 and the spring of 1965 brought a torrent of proposals to resolve the redwoods wrangle. First was the national park plan. Then Governor Edmund G. Brown stepped into the act with an even broader proposal, taking still more private forests but adding them to existing state parks. The American Forestry Association tossed in its recommendations: form a national park, but place it in the present Humboldt Redwoods State Park, "rounding out" existing acreage, and adding a few outstanding groves, such as the Tallest Trees, on Redwood Creek. (State Resources Administrator Hugo Fisher commented he saw no advantage in trading state signs for Federal "if you have exactly what you had before.")

This stump was a mature redwood
tree last year. Then it was felled.
Tenacious of life, the roots have
pushed up sprouts (foreground, rear)
which in time will become big trees,
true to their name. Sempervirens
means ever-living.

Cross section of a 126-year-old redwood, illustrating how "thinning" encouraged it to grow. Each ring represents one growing year. Under conditions of fierce competition with its neighbors, it grew slowly to one foot in diameter in 85 years (center dark section). In 1910, the surrounding timber was cut. Released to drink up sufficient light and air, tree then grew at 55 times the original rate to reach diameter of 4½ feet by 1951, when it was felled.

Ten years before this photo was made, this Pacific Lumber Company "residual" forest looked very much like the one on the opposite page. New trees from seeds and stump sprouts have filled the gaps left by cutting the larger trees. "Residuals" themselves have accelerated their growth.

On April 5, 1965, the redwood lumbermen made their own proposals: they offered to sell the state 8,000 acres of the finest remaining trees, and also to open another 260,000 acres in Del Norte, Humboldt, and Mendocino counties to "controlled" public recreation. The latter proposal reverses traditional industry policy against recreation on its lands for fear of liability and fires. Belated or not, the offers showed that the timber firms were willing to pay this price for state support against the national park.

Indeed, an important conflict-within-the-conflict, as Professor Fritz puts it, is, "Who should administer redwood parks? the state, which has done a fine job, or the Federal Government, which claims but cannot prove it can do better?"

Inexorably, the rising tide of tourism demands more room to flow in, and the Redwood Empire is feeling the pressure. Some preservationists argue tourism can take up the economic slack if logging is banned. Yet today's five million tourists supply less than a fifth of the region's dollars, and 15 million visitors are not foreseeable—at least for a while.

Secretary Udall estimates California's demands for outdoor recreation will require nine times today's available space within 50 years. Short of preempting every last forest, public and private, could California—or the Federal Government—satisfy such a demand?

Emanuel Fritz suggests:

"The nub of the problem lies in too many people. It would be more sensible for the Sierra Club to devote its efforts to controlling the increase of population. Only in that way can we be reasonably sure that what we save today for the inspiration of future generations is indeed saved."

Dr. William E. Siri, president of the Sierra Club, apparently agrees. Biophysicist Siri told the club's biennial Wilderness Conference in April, 1965, that expanding population is the prime threat to wilderness preservation. However Dr. Siri said he sees hope that America's population will stabilize at around 310 million a century hence, possibly when Americans become educated to prefer smaller families.

Meantime the Redwood Empire continues as a land of paradoxes: lumbermen cutting trees to save forests, wilderness-lovers fencing off public woods and demanding birth control, engineers bulldozing hillsides to bring people closer to beauty, governments competing for the right to administer a park that local interests oppose. . . .

227

Partnership of timberlands and recreation. Forester is measuring growth of a big redwood on land set aside for public enjoyment by one lumber company beside the Van Duzen River in central Humboldt County. Tourists are denied access to most actively operated private woodlands for reasons of safety. Recently more than 360,000 acres in forests like this, reserved against cutting, have been opened to public use.

Tree Farm sign (left) indicates this forest is under scientific management aimed at producing continual redwood "crop." Almost a quarter-century old, Tree Farm program embraces 60 million acres of private timberlands all over the United States. Property pays taxes, is subject to industry policing. Contrary to public conception, very little actual "planting" of redwoods is done. Mostly the program takes advantage of redwood's hardy propensity to renew itself, given the opportunity. In 1966 there were 750,000 acres in redwood tree farms, often rivaling parks in beauty.

Greatest enemy of redwoods and other forests continues to be fire. Air photo, near Orleans. Says Professor Emanuel Fritz: "In 1936, we had a series of bad fires in the redwood forests. Since then the industry and the State Division of Forestry have united in providing active protective and suppression services, with stations and equipment scattered throughout the forest regions. As a result, we haven't had a major redwood blaze since 1945."

Ground crews from State Division of Forestry hustle to blot out this fire in young pine and fir country near Orleans.

*Splintered and blackened, these stubs bear testimony
to destructiveness of a fire of long ago in the
northern Redwood Empire. Says Professor Fritz: The
Indians used to set fires to clear brush and make
more feed for deer and other game. For many years,
logging interests believed "it was healthy to have a
certain amount of fires," but the damage of 1936
caused a reversal of this thought.*

230

Compromise on the King

If there is to be a meeting point for conservationists, lumbermen, and campers, it may be in the King Range.

In this wild, almost untouched jumble of peaks and coast south of Cape Mendocino, the embattled interests are taking a cautious look at multiple use of wilderness land.

Traditionally the preservationists oppose commercial incursions into such pristine spots. Even campers are suspect: their cars and cookfires disturb the peace.

But at King Range, the Sierra Club for once finds common ground with ranchers, lumber operators, and ordinary recreationists. The club has endorsed King Range for multiple use.

The Department of the Interior's Bureau of Land Management views King Range as a pilot project that can provide both public recreation and private profit. The Bureau of Land Management already administers 31,500 acres of forest and mountainside there, and has built 34 primitive campsites. From its Ukiah office it also will supervise selective logging in the area, with revenues earmarked for road development and for recreation facilities. The bureau intends to reforest cutover sections, manage fish and game, and preserve scenery. Ultimately purchases will increase the Bureau's domain to 53,000 acres, make King Range a National Conservation Area.

The theory being tested is that—with wise and flexible supervision—man's recreation needs and his economic requirements can exist side by side. The theory is both challenging and hopeful.

Along all of its meandering thousand miles, California's coastline supports highways and towns. Except in the King Range. Thirty miles north of Fort Bragg, the coast road admits defeat and turns inland to avoid terrifying gorges and mountains that rise 4,000 feet out of the sea.

Men have tried to wring a living from the King, but few have succeeded. Its scenic grandeur is almost unmarred. Along this forbidden coast, barely scratched by logging roads, firs and redwoods tower and steelhead breast almost inaccessible streams. Deer and bear roam at will. Offshore fish proliferate, undisturbed by the West's mounting tide of sports fishermen.

The King's only town is Petrolia, where oil was discovered on the banks of the Mattole in the 1860's. Governor Leland Stanford's Mattole Petroleum Company drilled down a thousand feet for crude. This was California's pioneer strike, but it petered out. After 60 wells had been drilled, oil still came up slowly and in dribbles. There were few shipments, though gas seepage was piped to run a few cookstoves and light nearby farmhouses. Remnants of the old derricks can still be seen in a few places near Petrolia, overgrown with blackberry brambles.

Near Petrolia live descendants of Osawatomie John Brown. His widow Mary came west with the surviving children after the bearded abolitionist was hanged at Harpers Ferry in 1859.

*King Peak towers
4,087 feet a few miles
from the ocean.*

Smaller crossroads back of King Range include the post office and general store at Honeydew; and Ettersburg, where Albert Etter homesteaded in '94 and founded a famous seed-apple business. The Etters shipped apples to market by schooner from the mouth of the Mattole.

Shelter Cove, 25 miles west of Garberville, is the sports-lovers' destination in the King wilderness. In the protective hook of Point Delgada, once a galleon's landmark, there is a sandy beach for fishermen, clammers, and waders—in happy contrast to the dangerous coast above and below.

There is an airstrip at Shelter Cove, and a small store. Sportsmen from the Sacramento Valley fly over in summer and fall to spend the day fishing or hunting. Hollywood money plans a big vacation-home development nearby, with or without the approval of the Bureau of Land Management. Hundreds of lots already have been sold.

Shelter Cove and the King Range represent a green hope in the West, whose population explosion has already scarred recreation areas that are too easy of access.

King Range's sheer dip to the Pacific is shown in this aerial photo, looking south. Cape in the distance is Point Delgado. Road builders found the coast impassible here, left it to the deer.

Water tower and artists' quarters, Mendocino.

Old Baptist Church, enclosed water tower, Mendocino.

*The mountains march south
from Shelter Cove, wreathed in
morning mist.*

233

Cataclysm: December, 1964

There were signs and portents during the late summer and fall of 1964.

Rains came early, dampening the upper watersheds of the Eel and Klamath rivers, the national forests of the Yolla Bolly and Six Rivers wilderness.

Bears were seen in unprecedented numbers along the Klamath, their coats already heavy in September and October. Tiny green frogs appeared high in the firs and redwoods, just as they had before the epic floods of 1955. An old Hoopa woman who specialized in weather predictions advised her disciples that the winter of 1964–1965 would be worse than the "yardstick" one nine years earlier that flooded the Eel River bottomlands and the town of Klamath.

In November, heavy rains preceded exceptionally early snows in the basins of the Eel, the Klamath, and the Smith. November rainfall at Eureka was 160 percent of normal, highest since 1926. This pattern continued into December, saturating the ground like a sodden sponge. Meteorologists nervously watched while a disaster took shape. Their maps were carbon copies of 1955.

Just after midmonth, the Pacific High, a mass of high-pressure air which normally lies off the California Coast, protecting it from ocean-born tropical storms, suddenly split and moved north and south. Through the gap rushed a giant stream of moisture-laden warm air, dashing itself against the lofty Coast Ranges in the Siskiyous, the Trinities, and the mountains of coastal Oregon.

The rains began in earnest on Friday, December 18. Rain and snow continued on Saturday. On Sunday, December 20, the downpour intensified, washing away the earlier snowpacks and running off the mountain soil, now too soggy to absorb more moisture. Tiny creeks, normally easy to step across, swelled to torrents a hundred feet wide, carrying huge trees and boulders downstream. In the Six Rivers National Forest, whole mountains melted, adding seas of liquid mud to the downrushing mass. Thousands of creeks added an intolerable burden to the rivers in their narrow canyons. At Alderpoint, on the main fork of the Eel, the water level rose 90 feet. It is two feet deep in summer.

Gales whipped the coast on Monday, and the rains grew heavier. The rising rivers poured toward the sea, alarms were sounded, and by Monday night the small towns of Klamath, Pepperwood, Holmes, Weott, and Myers Flat were being evacuated. At Pepperwood, in an elbow where the Eel makes a wide flat turn, 82-year-old Henry Millsap started moving furniture upstairs. "Grandpa" Millsap had gone through four big floods at Pepperwood, including the one in 1955 when his lower rooms took water; and earlier in 1915, when his mother was rescued by skiff from an upper window. As the water continued to rise Monday night, Henry Millsap finally yielded to arguments, left in a power boat with his grandson John Hower for high ground.

En route, Millsap and Hower tried to reach Van's Café, where five neighbors had taken refuge. Mrs. Florence Porter, Mrs. Aletha Van Noy, Mr. and Mrs. Les Brueks and their crippled son Kelly had declined evacuation. They had stayed through 1955 they said, and they would take their chances. Now the Eel was making a new channel, and Hower's boat could not breast it.

Incredibly, the storm increased. On Tuesday alone, 11 inches of rain was measured at Richardson Grove State Park, on the Eel near the Mendocino County line. "Gully busters" washed out Highway 101 in several places, while the cross-mountain routes—199, 299, State Route 36—were rendered impassable from mud slides and slipouts. Water surged through Klamath, Orick, Myers Flat, and Weott, in some places 30 feet deep. The rivers were cresting as never before in man's memory. By noon on Tuesday, the 1955 high-water mark had been surpassed at Fernbridge, near the Eel's mouth, and debris-laden waves were washing across dairy farms and highways. The Eel was a filthy, foaming cascade, carrying a million cubic feet of water seaward every second—40 times the average flow of the mighty Sacramento at the state capital, three-quarters of the Mississippi's volume.

Sometime on Tuesday night the big bridges began to go. A listener at Rio Dell described the fall of the two-million-dollar Mudgett Memorial span as a long continuous groan—its tortured metal crying in the dark as trees smashed and wrenched its piers and abutments. Finally there was a high-pitched crack. The Eel had prevailed, and more than 600 feet of bridge vanished.

*The Eel had dropped a foot or more when this air photo was made about
2 P.M. on Wednesday, December 23. Looking south along submerged
Highway 101 south of Fortuna, lens catches matchstick pattern of logs from
a local mill's "cold deck," water cascading across highway, broken Mudgett
Memorial Bridge over the main channel, isolated town of Rio Dell.*

Between Rio Dell and the mill town of Scotia, the river slashed away 60 feet of bridge approach, isolating Rio Dell. Out went the lights, off went drinking water, power, gas, telephone. The town of 3,000 was to be cut off from land transport for more than two weeks; its main street (Highway 101) became a landing strip for light planes.

South of Scotia, the new Fleisher Memorial Bridge fell. Its 34-year-old neighbor span withstood the battering, though trees lodged in its girders 15 feet above the roadway. Farther south, railroad and highway bridges were crumpling all that day and night. The toll in major bridges alone would come to 18. One at Dyerville survived a logjam only because a state workman lowered himself into the pulsating mass with dynamite to blast it free. Up on the Klamath the 40-year-old Douglas Memorial Bridge lost half its length, and the town of Klamath disappeared. Water tore away 20 million board feet of logs at The Pacific Lumber Company yards in Scotia, whirled great battering rams downstream.

Wednesday was December 23, for those who cared. Rain continued, though now it seemed to diminish. At Richardson Grove that day, only a little over seven inches fell. At Fernbridge, the Eel appeared to have crested early Wednesday somewhere around 30 feet—the stream gauge could not be reached. By 2 P.M. it was back to 28 feet (11 above flood stage) and rescuers began to take heart.

Dwight O'Dell, publisher of the *Humboldt Beacon* at Fortuna, took off in a light plane to survey the floods. He flew south as far as Weott and reported scenes of devastation. Pepperwood was identifiable only as a pile of kindling—logs and smashed houses. Van's Café and its five occupants had disappeared. Four bodies were found days later, enmeshed in the rafters. The river had gone 10 feet over their refuge. Down in the Ferndale bottoms, drowned dairy cattle bobbed mournfully against barbed-wire fences.

Helicopters performed rescues from housetops, but at a terrible price. On Tuesday, during the storm's fury, a Coast Guard "chopper" picked up Mrs. Marie Bahnsen, Mrs. Bette Lee Kempf, and Mrs. Kempf's tiny daughter Melanie from a stricken farm near Ferndale, started toward Arcata Airport. Circling in rain and fog, the hovering craft smashed into woods north of the airport, killing all aboard, including three crewmen and a civilian "spotter," Arnold Hansen. Another volunteer "spotter," former County Supervisor Ervin Hadley, was lost December 26. He died with three servicemen when a Marine Corps helicopter from the U.S.S. *Bennington,* one of a score on emergency duty from the carrier's deck, crashed into the Eel near South Fork. The pilot, Captain Richard Gleason, escaped by inflating his Mae West life jacket, and was recovered after floating two miles downstream.

Marooned for 2½ days in the attic of their home at Grizzly Bluffs, dairyman Tony Leonardo signals to hovering aircraft as John Nunes watches through hole cut in the roof. Ten people were trapped under the rafters on the morning of December 22, lived on one can of fruit cocktail until rescued by boat on Christmas Eve. Floating logs and huge trees swirled across the Nunes and Leonardo dairy farms and pounded their refuge during most of the ordeal.

Left: *As floodwaters subside on the Klamath River, wreckage of the town of Klamath takes shape. Only the shell of Tony Ramos' grocery stands on the main street. Motels, stores, homes—all were swept away on the wild night of December 22–23. At top of photo, Douglas Memorial Bridge, which had carried Highway 101 since 1926, lost its south spans and north approach. Klamath will rebuild—but not here.* Right: *A mercy mission that boomeranged. Seven persons died in the crash of this Coast Guard helicopter as it tried to maneuver in a howling gale toward the Arcata airport. Three of the victims had been rescued from a marooned farmhouse near Ferndale minutes earlier.*

The agony was protracted by continuing bad weather. Relief and rescue planes were grounded for long periods. Despite this, Arcata's modest airport, built for fog-dispersal experiments during World War II, logged 433 planes a day during the crisis; tiny Rohnerville and Murray fields served almost as many. Waiting for rescue at Christmastime, families like that of Kathleen Mendes of Ferndale spent days and nights marooned in their attics. "We had a ham and a quart of whiskey, and it made teetotalers of the kids," she reported. At Stafford, Harriet Williams and her 12 children were evacuated by helicopter. It took two trips.

Disaster was compounded at Orleans when the schoolhouse caught fire December 22 and burned down with most of the town's salvaged clothing, bedding, and food inside. Isolated Orleans, fishing town on the upper Klamath, was without power and electricity for more than six weeks.

If people suffered and died, so did animals. Nearly 5,000 prime dairy cattle perished in the Eel bottoms. One rancher consented to be taken away in a boat only when his cows were up to their mouths in rising water. Friends said, "He didn't look back." After the floods, cattle bodies with Ferndale brands were found at Tillamook, 500 miles north on the Oregon Coast. One Black Angus steer survived by a miracle. He was swept down the Klamath and out to sea on a tangled raft of debris. Later he was spotted, shaky but alive, riding his impromptu *Kon-Tiki* in the littered harbor of Crescent City, 30 miles to the north. Compassionate townspeople made a plank road and rescued the half-dead beast, and Dave Stewart took charge of the steer with the remark: "He's earned his chance to live."

Finally the rains stopped. Most of January and February was fair; and the battered people could catch their breath, take stock.

The Redwood Empire took awhile lifting its head out of the mud. People who had watched their homes float away now stood around dazed—and bankrupt. Normal insurance doesn't cover "acts of God" like floods. Coming nine years to the day after the disaster of 1955, the new trauma seemed unbearable. But Federal and state aid was on the way, Red Cross and Salvation Army teams were on hand, and sympathetic neighbors lent a hand to clean out the mire.

237

Pepperwood and Klamath were gone, probably never to be rebuilt. Highway crews worked around the clock, restoring roads and building temporary bridges. State Highway Engineer Sam Helwer termed the road-restoration program "greatest in California history." This was the key: until the Redwood Highway and its east-west tributaries were rebuilt, only air traffic could move into Humboldt and Del Norte. Helwer thought it might take two to three years to fix all the damage, $35 million worth, but only a few months to make the principal routes passable for passenger cars. The Northwestern Pacific Railway was in worse shape, its tracks washed out for 50 miles in the steep Eel gorge, three bridges shattered, tunnels clogged with mud and trees. President "Charlie" Neal surveyed the losses, got the green light to start his $10 million rebuilding job. Since NWP carries 75 percent of the north's forest products, this was welcome news.

With big mills like Pacific Lumber badly damaged, shipping routes cut, and millions of feet in lumber washed downstream, heavy unemployment loomed. Pacific and its sister mills began the drudgery of picking up logs and finished lumber from the beaches south of Eureka and in Crescent City Harbor, where an estimated $15 million worth had washed up. Some of the logs were marked with the mill names; poachers reportedly put their own tags on a few. (A big redwood log is worth $1,000.) Farmers were happy to see the timber "blanket" rolled back so they could start restoring their fields and homes.

Effects of the rivers' catharsis were noted miles out to sea. Off Crescent City, a pilot reported a vast millpond: a mass of floating logs eight miles long and three miles wide. On the beaches south of Crescent City, late January produced a pall of smoke as debris burned.

Even as Humboldt and Del Norte counties were assessing damage, and hunting for bodies, preservationists returned to the fray, claiming the floods had been magnified by logging. Martin Litton, a magazine editor, wrote the San Francisco *Chronicle* that Redwood Creek "stained the ocean for miles with the soil of what had been a great forest," while nearby "an unlogged stream flowed into the sea, crystal-clear and scarcely increased in volume from its mid-summer flow." Litton asserted dams would not prevent the floods, and he advocated "restoring the forest cover to the steep slopes and then leaving it alone."

In the same newspaper on January 9, author Harold Gilliam also blamed much of the flood effect on pernicious logging. "Was this the greatest flood in a thousand years? Probably not," Gilliam said, adding: "In the flood itself . . . advocates of the proposed Redwood National Park had perhaps their most powerful argument."

Where once a town lived and breathed. . . . Pepperwood, 40 miles south of Eureka, has no recognizable landmarks left by 2 P.M. Wednesday, December 23. Houses, cafés, motels—all were swept in tangled wreckage into the woods when the Eel swept over the flats. Highway 101 lies under 10 feet of water in foreground.

Coast Guardsmen rescue a young flood victim near Fernbridge (left). Men in boats took scores of families from river-menaced farms.

Weott on Wednesday afternoon, 12 hours after the flood crest. South fork of the Eel (foreground) went completely over stores and homes, left six feet of silt in the streets. Highway 101 at top.

239

Flood's toll in broken communications begins to be measured at the end of Christmas Week, 1964. Utility crews inspect torn highway and shattered north end of the Mudgett Memorial Bridge, near Rio Dell.

Rampaging creek still cascades across broken Avenue of the Giants south of Weott two weeks after storm subsided. Miles of highway were swallowed in the disaster of late 1964 in the Humboldt–Del Norte region.

Typical of the destruction wrought on Northwestern Pacific Railroad in the Eel gorges was this stretch of track near Scotia Bluffs. Right-of-way slipped into the river for 50 miles.

After the river fell upon Pepperwood, homes and businesses were grotesquely tangled. At top, the Holmes & Holmes store upended in a clump of redwoods; at bottom, a house rests on a ruined motel.

241

Opponents pointed out that there was record precipitation and runoff on the headwaters of the Eel and the Klamath, which rise in national forest lands, where logging is closely supervised, and where no national park is advocated. The downpour in the redwood flats, where the park is proposed, had practically no effect on the overwhelming end product. Prairie Creek, heart of one park proposal, lies entirely outside the ravaged watersheds of the Eel and the Klamath, and the monster trees on Redwood Creek suffered no damage whatever, despite a logged hillside opposite.

Forest historians looked back to 1862 and found reports of an even more destructive flood, well before any significant logging. William H. Brewer, a Yale professor, told of this epic winter in his journal, saying men could traverse the whole San Joaquin Valley in a boat; and that Redwood Empire rivers brought an estimated million cords of logs and trees onto the beaches, equivalent to a half-billion board feet of lumber on one 10-mile stretch. According to Federal foresters' estimates, about 60 million board feet came down six affected streams in Christmas Week, 1964.

Typical of $32 million worth of damage to highways in the Redwood Empire during Christmas Week, 1964, was this 300-foot slipout on 101 west of Cummings, in northern Mendocino County. Motel cabin clings to far brink. On December 22, Squaw Creek swelled and tore out a ravine 100 feet deep. It was two weeks before emergency jeep roads could be bulldozed in this location; the devastation was repeated in a dozen spots between Cummings and Garberville, 30 miles north.

242

Barn rests on driftwood in a famous redwood grove south of Pepperwood. It formerly occupied a site at Larrabee, across the Eel River. Highway 101 (foreground) has been cleared for emergency travel in this photo made two weeks after the floods.

Mrs. Agnes Johnson's home in Weott weathered the 1937, 1955, and 1960 floods, but 1964's torrent carried it 100 yards to dump it atop a motel.

"Commercial timber operations could not have materially contributed to the terrible damage," the state forester reported on January 19. Lieutenant General Walter K. Wilson, chief of the U.S. Army Corps of Engineers, inspected the damage and concluded: "No amount of forestry practices can take care of a flood of that magnitude. The only answer would be a major reservoir system. As far as floods in a limited basin are concerned, that's as much of a whopper as I've ever seen."

The Sierra Club and its allies consider such statements self-serving. In his February, 1965, message to Secretary of the Interior Stewart Udall, President Johnson directed the Secretary to continue studies for a Redwood National Park.

Whereupon the Del Norte *Triplicate* remarked:

"Del Norte and the redwood region have had enough of natural disasters. We certainly cannot stand a 'government disaster.'"

Don Quinn's new $30,000 home at Myers Flat was buried under logs and mud when the Eel swept through town on December 21–22. Unbelievably, several plate-glass windows remained unbroken.

Drowned cows await mass burial on
the beach south of Humboldt Bay.
More than 2,000 were interred in
a single day to avoid epidemic.

The harbor of Crescent City was
solid with logs and debris for weeks
after the Christmas floods. Rivers
to the south deposited logs weighing
400 tons on the beaches here.
Their ownership presented a
knotty legal problem.

All-out efforts after the 1964 floods at last restored communications. Damage was reckoned in the hundred millions, and regions like Humboldt County were cut off from land transport for a month, but the Redwood Empire made a strong comeback. Above, the broken bridge at Klamath is almost repaired early in March. A ferry carried thousands of cars and trucks to keep the lifeline open until this span was completed on March 15.

The massive slipout near Cummings was restored to this condition by early March. Highway 101 (The Redwood Highway) had been opened to emergency traffic late in January in what was termed the greatest repair job in California history.

Improvisation, as for example this log bridge, reopened highways while permanent repairs began. Scene is at Redway on the Eel River.

246

A wartime Bailey Bridge spans the Smith River east of Crescent City on Highway 199. Millions were made available to the devastated counties for repairs like this, and another $57 million came from California motorists when the legislature voted to impose an extra penny gasoline tax, statewide, for nine months to aid the stricken region. Some "poison-oakers" said the floods gave Redwood Empire highways a ten-year boost.

Mudgett Memorial Bridge was reopened in May. Wreckage of old span, foreground.

Del Brush cleans out remains of home at Pepperwood, prepares to reopen his gift shop. Red Cross gave him a new trailer to live in.

An Empire Awakening: Some Glimpses of the Future

This is the story of a vaster Walden, one which can escape the fate of Thoreau's pond.

Its first popular discovery came as the aftermath of California's Gold Rush. Then mountainous terrain barred access. The northwest corner of the state slumbered for a century.

Today's rediscovery is stirring deep responses. America, especially the American West, is space hungry. Development is coming to the Redwood Empire, and wisdom is needed to cope with it.

Where redwoods punch a Big Hole in the Sky, as the old loggers put it, the New Conquistadores have found a place to uncoil from urban tensions. So far, the land's dimensions have proved generous enough to absorb those who appreciate it. Its recreation resources are barely tapped. Atop a ridge in Mendocino County, or beside a tributary of the roiling Smith, man is as remote from the Age of Anxiety as was Francis Drake. Sonoma, which had more inhabitants than Los Angeles in the 1850's, and is today only a 40-minute drive from San Francisco, still looks like a sleepy pueblo.

These are qualities of value in the exploding West. Can the Redwood Empire preserve them? Stanford Research Institute thinks geography will help for a while. Recently SRI computers split California into segments, predicted that the region north of the Golden Gate would grow slower than any. Another study estimates it will be 1975 before a million people live there . . . and by then California's population will top 24 millions.

With such big neighbors, pressures for *lebensraum* must mount. The redwood country will be coveted, exploited. Talking to North Coast county supervisors in January, 1964, Economic Consultant Stuart P. Walsh foresaw water replacing timber as the region's great treasure. "What you must decide," said Walsh, "is whether you will export it, or use it at home for industry and recreation." There are signs that arid Southern California wants water from the Eel, the Klamath, and the Trinity. And that end of the state has the votes. . . .

Walsh warned that land-planning is badly needed to preserve regional assets. Second-home tracts already have sprung up in the southern empire; unless carefully planned and strictly zoned, these pose a threat to scenic and economic values. Roadside stands and garish signboards have been sharply criticized for years, but zoning is a touchy political issue at the grass roots, and little legislation has been adopted to curb these desecrators.

Second home, on the Sonoma Coast at Timber Cove. Several of these contoured colonies are under construction.

248

Visitors a-coming, or commuters going home—the Golden Gate Bridge is at designed capacity, carrying 27 million vehicles a year. Built in 1937 by its neighbor counties without a cent of state or Federal funds, the bridge now looks for expedients to carry more traffic at peak hours, and its directors have concluded a lower deck is needed.

249

Suburban delight. A redwood home perches beside a canyon in Mill Valley, a 15-minute commute from San Francisco —but not in peak traffic hours of morning and evening.

Neptune's gospel, that water is the primary resource, has its disciples. The State of California, in a report on North Coast recreation issued in March, 1965, ties water and fun tightly together. "Sixty percent of all recreation in California is water-oriented," says this survey. "No reservoir, no lake, no stream is too remote to be used."

In terms of water, the Redwood Empire is wildly rich. As yet its lakes, rivers, and seacoast are barely developed. This is due in part to the short, June-to-September tourist season, in part to lack of promotion and risk capital. Now there are signs that this is changing: well-financed resorts and second-home colonies have appeared since 1960. A San Francisco syndicate has sunk several millions into Steele Park, on new Lake Berryessa—a marina-centered resort. On the northern Sonoma Coast, Honolulu money has decreed a stately leisure-time community of split-level homes, golf courses, and condominiums. Another is in prospect near Napa. If these succeed, others will follow.

A dual bonus lies in development of the inland water resource. Floods wreaked havoc down the valleys of the Eel and the Klamath twice in 10 years. Yet when funds are available, floods can be curbed with dams. Dams produce reservoirs. And, in California, reservoirs provide the ultimate in recreation: predictable fishing, boating, water-skiing. The State Department of Parks and Recreation says that of its 104 park units, the four built around big reservoirs account for one-eighth of all public attendance.

Plans are afoot to tame the Eel with a ladder of flood-control dams. Potentially this dovetails with proposals to divert Eel River water into Clear Lake, and eastward, for irrigation. Costly and ambitious, these projects are some years from reality, so the Redwood Empire still has time to chart its course, and its new discoverers have time to indulge their imagination.

But in the last third of the twentieth century, nobody slumbers very long.

The redwood country is on the verge of waking.

Eastern Marin County, its bay and its bridges.
Proximity to San Francisco (in distance at top)
virtually assures that Marin's population will
triple in the next two decades.

Beyond all, beauty endures.
Humboldt beaches south
of Trinidad Head.

. . . and nature imparts
peace and introspection.

Index

Alaska, 94
Albert, King of Belgium, 63
Albertson, Eric, 122
Albion, 106, 114, 116, 122; — Woods, 105; — Mill, 112; — River, 112; — River Railroad, 114; — Wharf, 116
Alderpoint, 234
Altimira, Fray José, 26, 28
American Forest Products Industries, 222, 223
American Forestry Association, 226
American President Lines, 121
Among the Redwoods in California, 180
Anchor Bay, 93, 102
Anderson Valley, 144; — — Apple Show, 145
Antelope (side-wheeler), 90
apples, 232
Arbor Day (California), 63
Arcata, 215, 225; — Airport, 236
Archives of Shensi, 162
Arnold, General H. H. "Hap," 82, 83
Asti, 78, 79
Avenue of the Giants, 240

Bancroft, Hubert Howe, 46, 201
Bancroft Library (Berkeley), 25
Battery Point Lighthouse, 206
Bay Wind Gallery, 126, 128
Bear Flaggers, 47
Bear Flag Revolt, 45, 46, 50
Bear Harbor, 106
Beaulieu Vineyards, 72
Bell Springs Mountain route, 158
Belvedere, 31, 32
Bergen, County Sheriff Tom, 144
Beringer Brothers, 73; "Rhine House," 72; Roy Raymond, 77
Big Hole in the Sky, 248
Big Lagoon, 216
Big River, 27, 104, 105, 122
Big Sur, 127
Black Bart, 152, 153; — — Rock, 153
Bloody Island, 80
Board of Forestry, 216
boating, 34, 80, 87, 88; party-boat expeditions, 132
Bodega, 92; — County, 92
Bolinas, 32, 37
Bolton, Charles E.; see Black Bart
Boont Ling, 144, 145
Bothwell, Dorr, 127, 128
Bourn, William, 77
Bowman, Kent, 127
Brandon, Kenneth, 127
Brannan, Sam; Calistoga (founder), 66, 67; Spring Grounds Hotel, 67; *General Morgan,* 164; Brannan's Mendocino Company, 164
Branscom, 140
Brother Jonathan, 202, 203
Brown, Charlie, 130
Brown, Governor Edmund G., 218, 226
Bryan, William Jennings, 50
Bryce, Colonel Arthur T., 82
Buckaloo, Bill, 136

Buena Vista, 51, 54; Haraszthy mansion, 52; — Vinicultural Society, 53; — Winery, 84
Bufano, Benjamin, 100
Buhne, Hans Henry, 164, 165
Burbank, Luther, 62, 63
Bureau of Land Management, 219, 231, 232
Byce, Lyman C., 49
Byron, Lady, 61

Cabrillo, Captain Juan Rodriguez, 162
Cacafuego, 22
California: — Republic, 46; — art and artists, 127–129; — Historical Society, 146; — admitted to Union, 164; — maritime disasters, 202
California Redwood Manufacturing Company, 106
Calistoga, 68, 70, 72, 90; hops-growing, 79
Calistoga and Clear Lake Stage Company, 69
"Calorie Canyon," 98–99
Campa, Father, 166
Cape Mendocino, 162, 163, 231
Caperton, Rear Admiral William B., 190
Carpenter, Aurelius Ornando, 78, 80, 106, 110, 114, 130, 132, 148; Grace —, 146, 147
Carrillo, José Ramon, 27; — family, 44, 47
Carson, Rachel, 81
Carson, William, 216, 224; — mansion, 184, 185
Caspar, 106
Castro, Governor José, 44
cataclysm (1964), 234–247
Cermeño, 28, 119
Charles III, King, 162
Chevaillier, Alzire, 60
Chiang Kai-shek, 82
Childs, Judge John L., 200, 206
Chinese, 162; — labor, 77, 108; Hong-Tsi (San Francisco Bay), 162; Chinatown, 173
Christian Brothers, 72
Chrysopylae (Golden Gate), 21
Clark, Colonel Lawrence, 84
Clarke Museum (Eureka), 162, 167
Clayton, David, 127
Clear Lake, 65, 80, 83, 88, 142, 164; plumbers' paradise, 85
Clements, Dick, 100
Cleone, 106
Cleveland, President Grover, 179
Coast Gallery, 127
coast redwoods, 177
coastal inns, 135
Cobb Mountain, 83
Cobweb Palace, 136
Comstock Lode, 107
Contra Costa hills, 216
Cooke, Admiral Charles M., 82, 84
Coombs, Silas, 105
Covelo, 142; — Rodeo, 145

covered bridges, 199
Crabtree, Lotta, 90
Crescent City, 201, 204, 207; — — harbor, 245
Crespi, Fray Juan, 175
Crivelli, Babe, 201
Crocker, Charles, 67, 154
Crotty, Harry, 127
Cutter, Captain E. P., 51

Del Norte County, 204, 209, 227; first settlement, 154; Stout Tree, 217; — — woods, 212
Dennen, Loren, 135, 136
Department of the Interior, 231
"Devil's Elbow," 157
Dillon, Army Lieutenant Edward, 142
Dillon, Richard H., 190
Dillon Beach (Marin County), 42
Division of Highways, 217
Doctrine of 1823, 95
Dolbeer, John, 182
Dollar, Captain Robert, 121
Donohue's Landing, 90
Douglas, Congresswoman Helen Gahagan, 217
Douglas fir, 215
Drake, Sir Francis, 23, 28; "plate of brasse," 22, 25; — Bay, 22, 25; *Golden Hind,* 22; — Estero, 24, 25, 39; "New Albion," 22, 24; "heirs," 25; — Navigators' Guild, 25; Elizabeth I, 38
Dresel, Emil, 53
Dry Lagoon, 197
Durante, Jimmy, 81

East Bay Hills, 104
Edison, Thomas, 63
Eel River, 154, 155, 157, 162, 164, 181, 234–236, 239, 242–244, 246
Elizabeth I, 22
English, Buck, 69
English in California, 22–25; territorial claims, 25
Ericson, Augustus W., 111, 166, 173, 174, 180, 182, 183
Etter, Albert, 233; Ettersburg, 233
Eureka, 162, 165, 178, 184, 193
Evans, "Petrified Charlie," 70

Fairfax, Charles Snowden ("Lord Charlie"), 30
Falbrook, 198
Ferndale, 187
Figueroa, Governor José, 28, 44
Firestone, Harvey, 63
Fisher, Harrison, 58
Fisher, Hugo, 226
fishing, 87, 88, 192, 193, 210, 233; ocean trout, 130; steelhead, 130; salmon, 130–132, 189, 192, 210, 211; Noyo, 131, 132; dip netter, 139; surf smelt, 139; Juan Creek, 139; Dungeness crab, 189; salmon fleet, 211
Fleisher Memorial Bridge, 236

Fletcher, Chaplain Francis, 25; chronicle, 22
Font, Father, 216
Ford, Arnold, hop kiln of, 78
Ford, Ernie, 81
Ford, Henry, 63
Ford, Jerome, 106, 123
Forest Practices Act, 224
Fort Bragg, 105–108, 110–112, 115, 223
Fort Ross, 44, 71, 94, 95, 100, 120
Foss, Clark, 67, 70, 90
Fountain Grove, 60
Frémont, Captain John Charles, 21, 46
Fritz, Professor Emanuel, 222, 224–227, 229, 230

Garibaldi, Giuseppe, 90
Garcia River, 130
Gasquet, Horace, 200
Geyser Development Company, 90
Gibson, Lieutenant Horatio, 106
Glen Ellen, 55–58, 82
Gold Bluffs beach, 220
Gold Rush, 30, 66; see Brannan, Sam
Golden Gate, 21, 22, 29, 131; — — Bridge, 155; bridge construction, 30
Grant, President Ulysses S., 90, 170, 171
Greeley, Horace, 61
Greenwood, 106, 122
Gregg, Dr. Josiah, 164
Grosvenor, Melville Bell, 217
Grove Play (annual), 97
Grundeman, Forester Robert, 222
Gualala River, 130
Guenoc Ranch, 81
Guerne, George, 96
Guerneville, 97
Gundlach, Jacob, 53
Gunther Island, 162

Halleck, Henry, 29
Haraszthy, Count, 51–54, 72, 74; Nicaragua, 54
Harpending, Asbury, 154, 155
Harper, Harvey M., 156
Harris, Thomas Lake, 60, 61
Harte, Bret, 186, 187; Maggie, 186
Hatfield, Bob, 149
Hawthorne, Nathaniel, 61
Heald, Tom, 96
Healdsburg, 96
Hearst, William Randolph, 33
Heceta, Bruno de, 162
Heeser, August A., 123
Heritage House, 135, 136
Hervilla, Cora Coombs, 126
Hervilla, Ole, 135
highways, 201, 243, 247; Redwood Highway (Highway 101), 149, 156, 158, 159, 204, 205, 215, 217, 224, 234–236, 246; *California Highway Bulletin,* 156; *California Highways and Public Works Magazine,* 156; road construction, 156; Redwood Empire